A CARTOON HISTORY OF TH

Volume 2: The Dawn of Life

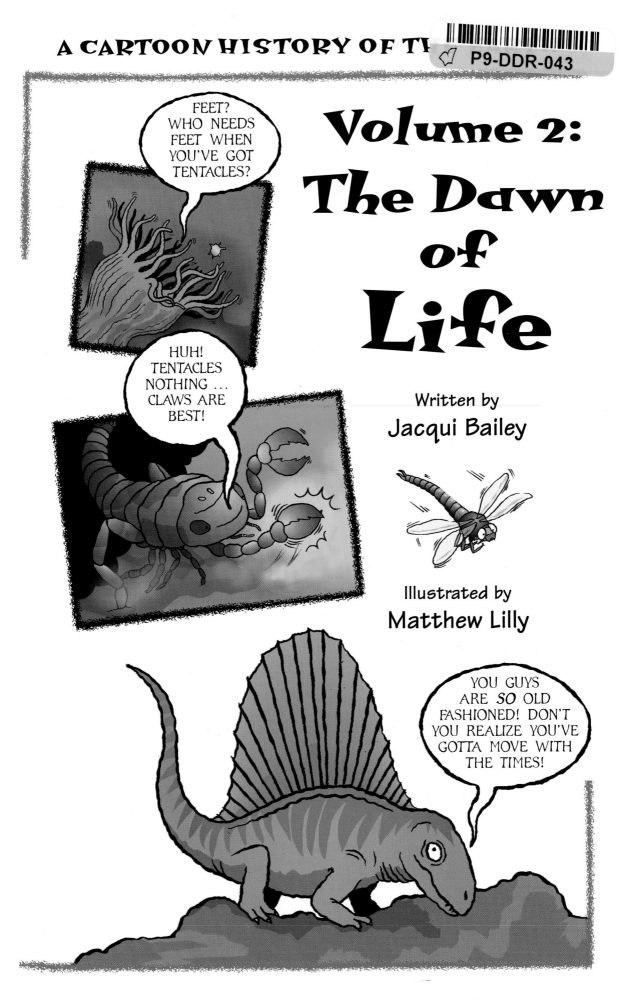

Written by
Jacqui Bailey

Illustrated by
Matthew Lilly

FEET? WHO NEEDS FEET WHEN YOU'VE GOT TENTACLES?

HUH! TENTACLES NOTHING ... CLAWS ARE BEST!

YOU GUYS ARE *SO* OLD FASHIONED! DON'T YOU REALIZE YOU'VE GOTTA MOVE WITH THE TIMES!

Kids Can Press

For Mum and Dad, with love
J. B.
For Polly
M. L.

With thanks to Martin Jenkins
for being so helpfully nit-picky!

Copyright © Two's Company 2001

Published by permission of A&C Black
(Publishers) Limited, London

Published in Canada by   Published in the U.S. by
Kids Can Press Ltd.   Kids Can Press Ltd.
29 Birch Avenue   2250 Military Road
Toronto, ON M4V 1E2   Tonawanda, NY 14150

www.kidscanpress.com

Printed in Hong Kong by
Wing King Tong Company Limited

The hardcover edition of this book
is smyth sewn casebound.

The paperback edition of this book is
limp sewn with a drawn-on cover.

CM 01 0 9 8 7 6 5 4 3 2 1
CM PA 01 0 9 8 7 6 5 4 3 2 1

Canadian Cataloguing in Publication Data

Bailey, Jacqui
The dawn of life
(The cartoon history of the earth ; 2)
Includes index.

ISBN 1-55337-072-4 (bound)
ISBN 1-55337-081-3 (pbk.)

1. Life – Origin – Comic books, strips, etc. –
Juvenile literature. I. Lilly, Matthew.
II. Title. III. Series: Bailey, Jacqui. Cartoon
history of the earth ; 2.

QH325.B34 2001   j576.83
C00-933320-7

NELVANA

Kids Can Press is a Nelvana company

As you read this book, you'll see some words in capital letters — **LIKE THIS**. These words are listed in the Glossary on pages 30–31, where there is more information about them. And when you see the asterisk (✳), look for a box on the page that also has an asterisk. This box gives you even more information on the topic.

A thousand million years ago, Earth wasn't anything like it is now. To begin with, absolutely nothing lived on land — not a bird, or a bug or a buttercup. There was just rubble and dust, and great rivers of solid black rock left over from erupting volcanoes.

All the big pieces of land — the CONTINENTS — were in the southern half of the world. The northern half was just one enormous ocean.✳

✳ The land and the oceans lie on top of the Earth's **CRUST**. Over millions of years the crust slowly moves about, and as it does so the land and the oceans move with it.

Back then, the ocean was definitely the place to be. It was *stuffed* with billions and billions of strange-looking life-forms.

Some had wriggling tails to push them along. Others had hairlike threads that rowed them through the water.

Some spun fancy shell-like shapes around themselves and floated about looking like ice-cream cones or helmets.

And some were just shapeless blobs of jelly that moved by pushing pieces of themselves forward.

We don't know very much about these life-forms, but one thing we're pretty sure of is that most were *incredibly* small.

In fact, they were mainly just single CELLS — little pieces of living stuff so tiny you or I wouldn't have been able to see them.

Then, around 800 million years ago, things changed. Suddenly bunches of cells started to get together in a big way — and bingo! Sponges had appeared! *

THERE! SEE WHAT YOU CAN DO WHEN YOU STICK TOGETHER!

* You wouldn't think so to look at them, but sponges are **ANIMALS.** In fact, they may have been the first animals to appear on Earth!

Once cells caught on to the idea of sticking together, there was no stopping them. By 650 million years ago, all kinds of strange creatures were appearing in the oceans.

Some stuck up from the sea floor and caught little bits of food that floated by.
   They looked more like plants than animals. There were sea anemones, with long waving fronds, and sea pens that grew as tall as gateposts and had hundreds of tiny branching arms.

sea pens

sea anemones

* Amazingly, these kinds of animals still exist in the oceans today — and they look pretty much the same now as they did then.

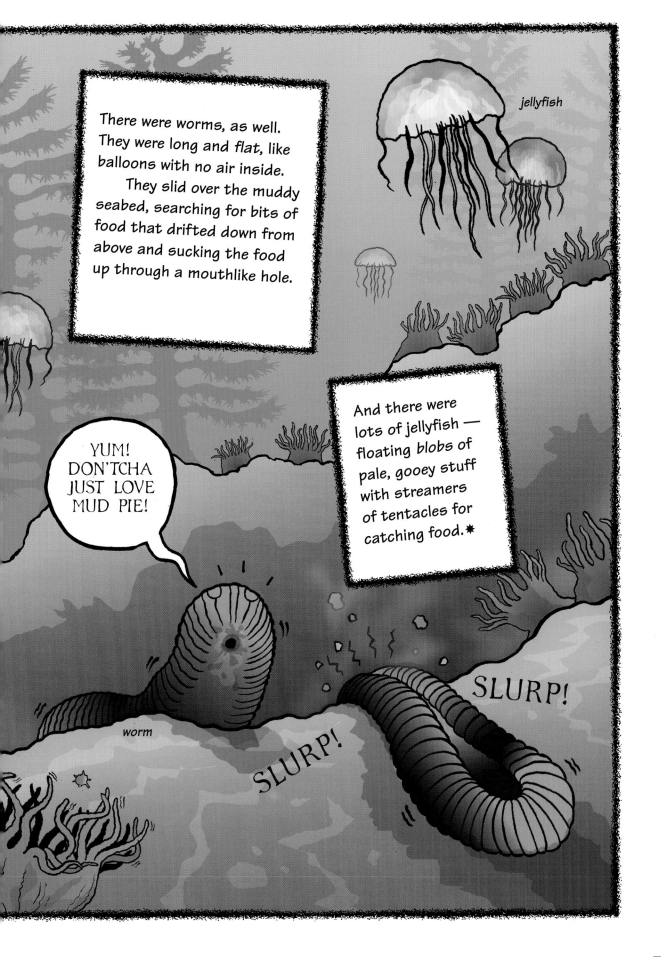

There were worms, as well. They were long and flat, like balloons with no air inside.

They slid over the muddy seabed, searching for bits of food that drifted down from above and sucking the food up through a mouthlike hole.

jellyfish

And there were lots of jellyfish — floating blobs of pale, gooey stuff with streamers of tentacles for catching food. ✳

YUM! DON'TCHA JUST LOVE MUD PIE!

worm

SLURP!

SLURP!

The big difference with these animals was that they didn't just have lots of cells — they had lots of *different types of* cells, and each type of cell had a *particular job.*

STUNNING SET OF TENTACLES YOU HAVE THERE, MY DEAR!

Jellyfish, for example, had muscle cells to move their bodies around, and digestive cells to break down their food. They even had special stinging cells in their tentacles for knocking out their PREY.

Life was getting *complicated!*

Wait a minute! How do WE know what life was like?

Good question! In fact, we're still finding out about it. There's still an awful lot we don't know, but most of what we do know has come from finding fossils.

Fossils are the remains of things that lived a very long time ago.

They might be formed from the bodies of dead animals and plants, or even from microscopic single cells.

Sometimes fossils just show the shape of something, like a footprint.

Some fossils are found inside amber.

Amber forms from a sticky tree juice, called resin. Sometimes resin leaks out of a tree and small animals get stuck in it. Then the resin dries into hard, glassy amber — with the animal still trapped inside.

The oldest amber fossils found so far date from about 100 million years ago. But there are other fossils that are much older than that ...

The oldest fossils are found inside rock. It happens something like this ...

Imagine that an animal dies and sinks to the bottom of the sea. If the seabed is sandy or muddy, the animal may get covered over. The soft pieces of its body usually rot away, but hard pieces, like bone or shell, might be left behind.

Thousands of years go by, and more and more sand and mud piles on top of the body.

The weight of it all gradually turns the muddy sand into rock, and the body pieces become fossils — stony models that look exactly like the body pieces once did.

Over millions of years, the Earth's surface changes. What was a seabed might become a mountain. ✷

✷ Movements in the Earth's crust can slowly fold up parts of the land or ocean floor into mountains.
But sometimes the land or the seabed is pushed underneath the crust instead.

Wind and rain wear away at the mountain, and gradually new layers of rock are brought to the surface. Buried in the rock are the fossils.

Nowadays, scientists and other people go looking for fossils. When they find one, they carefully chip away the rock around it. Then the fossil is taken to be cleaned and polished.

The fossil can be tested to find out how old it is (give or take a few million years). And by studying it, and comparing it to life-forms that exist today, a scientist can sometimes figure out what that fossil might once have been.

I'M OUTTA HERE! NOBODY'S GOING TO CALL ME AN OLD FOSSIL!

The problem is, only a few of all the life-forms that have ever lived end up as fossils.

They have to die in exactly the right sort of place for one thing. Then they have to be quickly covered up before they rot away completely. And then the rock they're buried in has to get pushed to the surface.

In fact, it's really quite amazing that we ever find any fossils at all!

Now where were we? Oh, yes ...

The next great change happened about 540 million years ago. All sorts of new animals suddenly burst on to the scene, and lots of them had tough skins or hard shells.

Life was starting to stiffen up!

One of the biggest hunters of the time was called Anomalocaris.✷ It was about half a meter (yard) long and had 11 pairs of finlike paddles along its body.

✷ When scientists discover a life-form they haven't seen before, they give it a scientific name in Latin or Greek.

Most plants and animals have a common name as well. For example, Helix aspersa is also called a garden snail. But fossils don't usually have common names so we have to use their scientific names.

YUM! DON'TCHA JUST *LOVE* JELLY!

It also had a round mouth full of sharp teeth and two odd-looking horn-shaped feelers — probably for stuffing food into its mouth!

Armored trilobites trundled over the ocean floor. Some were tiny, but others were as big as trash-can lids.

We think they vacuumed up the remains of dead animals or cells that drifted down from above. But some may have gobbled up live animals, too.

SLURP!

SLURP!

SLURP!

SLURP!

SO, WHADDYA THINK? IS IT SAFE TO OPEN UP YET?

Some small soft-bodied creatures soon discovered that shells meant safety.

Brachiopods had two shells that fit closely together. Groups of brachiopods clung to the seabed or to sponges.

When the coast was clear, they opened their shells to filter tiny bits of food from the water.

But when danger threatened, they snapped their shells tight shut!

Then there were the REAL odd-balls ...

Wiwaxia wasn't taking any chances. It covered itself with tough armored scales and spines.

PERSONALLY, I JUST *DON'T* SEE THE POINT OF *FIVE* EYES, DO YOU?

Hallucigenia was like a worm on stilts! It had 14 pairs of spines — seven on its back and seven underneath.

While *Opabinia* would look good in any science-fiction movie. It had *five* eyes, paddles all along its sides and a long tube-like trunk with sharp spines on the end. Luckily, it was only about 7 cm (2¾ in.) long!

For the next 100 million years, all kinds of creatures appeared in the oceans ...

Giant MOLLUSKS called nautiloids jetted around inside shells that looked like wizards' hats.
        Some were up to 9 m (10 yd.) in length — longer than two cars!

Smaller, snail-like mollusks crept through forests of tall, stalky sea lilies.

(Sea lilies are still around today. The "branches" of these odd-looking animals are covered with sticky tubes to trap bits of food that float by.)

And sea scorpions as big as crocodiles *lurked* in the shadows, ready to grab anything that strayed too close to their powerful claws.

FISH began to show up, too ...

At first, they were small and simple. They had no jaws or teeth, just a mouth hole for sucking up food. Many had a bony helmet over their head and bony scales on their tail.

They probably spent their time nosing around in the mud.

IF ONLY WE HAD SOME JAWS WE COULD CHEW THINGS OVER ONCE IN A WHILE.

There were fish with scales and fish with bony armor. Fish with jaws and fish without. Fish that lived on the seabed, and huge hunting fish that prowled the waters above!

But by 400 million years ago, things had changed. Most fish now had a skeleton, which could support strong muscles. They had GILLS for breathing, and movable jaws — some stuffed with sharp teeth!

Animals with BACKBONES had arrived, and for the next 50 million years or so, the world went *wild* with fish!

One of the largest was Dunkleosteus. It was as big as a bus! Its gaping jaws were lined with jagged plates instead of teeth, and armor plating covered its enormous head.

I ONLY SAID, "WHO WANTS TO PLAY?"

Lots of fish had bony skeletons — as most fish do today. But some had a skeleton made of cartilage. (Cartilage is lighter and more flexible than bone.)

One group of cartilage fish in particular had a fast streamlined body, large fins and row after row of sharp teeth. ✹ They were the first sharks!

EEEEEK!

✹ Unlike most of us, sharks never run out of teeth! If they lose some while they're chomping on a meal, new ones pop up to fill in the gaps. A shark can grow hundreds of teeth during its lifetime!

Meanwhile, back on land ...

North

Equator

South

While life was being so busy in the ocean, things were happening on land, too.

By 400 million years ago, movements in the Earth's crust had clumped most of the continents together and they were slowly drifting north.

Those same movements had pushed up mountains — which wind and rain had worn down again. Volcanoes had hurled out thick clouds of dust and ash. And the world's climate had changed and changed again.

Sometimes, the climate was so *cold* huge ice sheets spread across the Earth.✳ At other times, the land baked under a *hot* Sun.

✳ In the past, extreme changes in climate have sometimes caused vast numbers of different life forms to die out completely. Scientists call these events **MASS EXTINCTIONS**. They think there have been at least ten mass extinctions since life began.

As the continents collided, the sea level rose and fell. Great stretches of muddy shallows formed along the coasts. And it was here that the next major event took place ...

Around the time that the first animals were appearing in the sea, some single cells had got together to form ALGAE (seaweed to you and me).

Seaweeds usually dry out fast when they get washed ashore, but over the years something strange had happened ...

LAST ONE ON LAND'S A ROTTEN EGG!

Some types of seaweed had grown a waxy overcoat.

Now when they got washed ashore they *didn't* dry out so easily. They even began to grow on *land*!

At first these new life-forms grew close to the ground, as MOSSES AND LIVERWORTS do.

But before long, some of them had roots to suck up water from the mud ... stems to hold up their heads ... and a system of tubes for carrying food and water around inside them as they grew.

GOOD GRIEF! WHAT'S GOING ON UP THERE?

Most were only a few inches (centimeters) tall, but ... they were the *biggest* things on land. PLANTS had arrived!

Gradually plants moved inland. It was slow going, though. First they had to make soil to grow in — and soil is made from layers of *dead plants* mixed with sand and mud!

The new plants were also a new *source of food*, and before long they were followed onto land by animals — small, multi-legged creatures with tough, armored skins.

They were ARTHROPODS — mites, millipedes and wingless INSECTS. Their tough skins were waterproof, so they didn't dry out on land, but they did have to find ways of getting oxygen from the air instead of from water.

These first land animals were happy to munch on plants. But they were soon followed by other creatures who were more interested in munching on *them* — meat-eaters such as scorpions and centipedes!

By 360 million years ago, some plants had grown woody stems, fleshy leaves and long branching roots — trees had appeared.

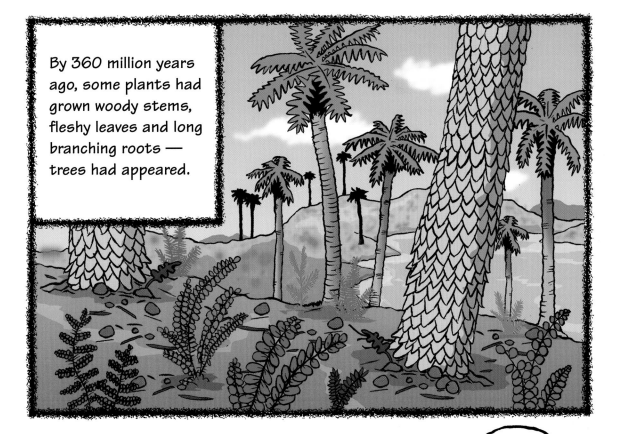

The world's weather was pretty warm around this time, and the muddy coastal shallows had turned into steamy swamps. Some of the fish that lived in these swamps began coming to the surface to take gulps of air.✳

PHEW! GIMME OXYGEN!

✳ Swamp water often holds less oxygen than sea water, so the fish must have found it hard to breathe.

In time, some of these fish developed LUNGS as well as gills. This meant they could take in oxygen from the air as easily as from water.

These lungfish swam with the help of stubby fins — one pair near the front of the body and the other toward the back.

Eventually the fins turned into stumpy *feet* that didn't just paddle the animal through the water, but also held up its heavy body on land.

The first "four-feet" were here. The age of AMPHIBIANS had begun!

NOW *I* RULE THE WORLD!

UH-OH! HERE WE GO AGAIN!

✱ This period in Earth's history is known as the Carboniferous period and it lasted from about 360 to 286 million years ago.

Most of the coal we burn in the world today was formed from layers of dead plants that grew during Carboniferous times.

Amphibians can live both on land and in water. These first ones lived in a world of hot, damp swamp-forests packed with *giant* plants that grew up to 45 m (50 yd.) high — taller than a ten-story building. ✱

The swamp-forests *hummed* with life. Spiders and centipedes scuttled over the ground, and millipedes up to 2 m (6 ft.) long munched on rotting leaves.

HMMMM!

WRRRR!

CHOMP!

MUNCH!

Insects had discovered how to fly. Cockroaches and dragonflies — some as big as pigeons — blundered through the trees.

Most amphibians had short, pointed teeth that were perfect for crunching up insects or fish. And as there was plenty of food, there were soon lots of amphibians, too.

Some were no bigger than hamsters, and probably fed on tiny water animals.

But others, like *Eogyrinus*, were monsters — some grew as long as two sofas!

SNAP!

For about 100 million years, life was good to the amphibians.
Then the world began to change. Amphibians really like to be around water, or somewhere damp at least.✳ But the weather was getting hotter again and some of the swamps began to dry up!

✳ Amphibians soak up water through their skin — many of them can't "drink" in any other way. Also, like lots of water animals, most amphibians lay soft, jellylike eggs that need water to support and protect them.

As the swamps shrank, a new type of animal came along. Its skin was tough and leathery and its body didn't lose water the way an amphibian's did.

WELL, *HELLO* THERE!

And its eggs had a shell that was *waterproof*!
The shell kept in all the food and liquid the baby animal needed, and guarded the egg from knocks and bumps. These eggs could be laid on dry land.

The REPTILES had arrived!

The amphibians and these early reptiles were probably "cold-blooded" animals (as amphibians and reptiles are today). This means they got going by soaking up heat from the Sun, instead of heating their bodies themselves.

I DON'T KNOW *WHERE* THEY GET THE ENERGY!

This wasn't a problem for reptiles. Their waterproof skin meant they could spend *lots* of time racing around in the sunshine without needing to find more water. The amphibians, on the other hand, had to stay in their shady swamps and take things easy.

WAKEY! WAKEY!

Reptiles known as "sail-backs" had a large fin on their back. They may have used it as a "sun-catcher" to help them warm up fast in the morning. By being the first to get going, they could grab their breakfast before it woke up!

Before long, there were reptiles *everywhere*. Big meat-eaters fed on smaller ones, and the smaller ones fed on whatever they could catch.

But not all reptiles were meat-eaters. Some of the biggest and the *ugliest* reptiles ate plants.

The strange-looking creature called *Moschops* was about the size of a cow, and it probably grazed like one, too.

Moschops

Smaller reptiles that looked a lot like lizards do today darted about snatching up insects, worms and snails.

Some had wing-flaps and could glide from tree to tree. Some even went back to living in the water!

THEN DISASTER STRUCK!

Around 245 million years ago, the world's climate changed so dramatically that millions of plants and animals *died out!*✳

✳ This period of Earth's history, from 286 to 245 million years ago, is called the Permian.
More than half of all the **SPECIES** of plants and animals in the world vanished in the mass extinction that took place at the end of the Permian — including nearly all of the life-forms in the sea. Scientists are still trying to find out what caused it.

It was the greatest mass extinction ever known — almost as if life was clearing the decks to start again ...

BUT THAT'S ANOTHER STORY!

Ages and Ages Ago

Scientists divide up the history of Earth into different "ages," each with its own special name. The only problem is, not all scientists agree about when each of these periods starts and finishes.

The dates and names of the ages covered in this book are listed below. You might find that some of these dates are a bit different in other books. Don't worry about it, though. They should be more or less the same — give or take a million years or so!

2500–544 mya✱ — PROTEROZOIC ERA

By 1200 mya — nothing lives on land, but the ocean is full of life-forms — mostly single cells.

By 800 mya — some cells have grouped together to make the first animals — sponges.

By 650 mya — other multi-celled animals have appeared, such as jellyfish and worms.

✱ mya stands for "millions of years ago."

544–245 mya — PALEOZOIC ERA

544–505 mya — Cambrian:
Shelled and armored animals and algae appear.

505–440 mya — Ordovician:
Giant mollusks and armored, jawless fish.

440–410 mya — Silurian:
Lots of trilobites, sea scorpions and early jawed fish. First true land plants appear.

410–360 mya — Devonian:
Lots of fish, including those with backbones. Plants spread inland, followed by first land animals — millipedes, scorpions, early insects and other arthropods.

360–286 mya — Carboniferous:
Huge swamp-forests, winged insects and lots of amphibians.

286–245 mya — Permian:
Lots of reptiles, seed plants and conifer trees.

Mass Extinction — many life-forms die out.

Life's a Puzzle

Putting together the story of life is like doing a giant jigsaw puzzle with half the pieces missing! One of the ways that scientists fill in the gaps is by studying fossils and comparing them to life-forms that exist today.

Fossils show us how the bodies of plants and animals have changed over millions and millions of years.

This process of gradual change is what we life-forms do best! It's called *evolution* and it's why spiders spin webs, giraffes have long necks and legs, and humans walk on two legs (most of the time).

HEY, STILTS! PASS DOWN A FEW LEAVES, WILL YA?

In 1859, a book called *On the Origin of Species* was written by a man named Charles Darwin to describe how he thought evolution worked. And he backed up his ideas with lots of information that he'd discovered over the years about different plants and animals.

I DON'T REMEMBER LIVING IN THE SEA!

Darwin believed that all living things have a hard job to survive. And those animals or plants (or cells) that survive *best* gradually replace the less successful types, which either die out altogether or find another way to live.

Darwin's book was a *sensation!* Some people thought it was garbage, but for many it helped to explain the enormous variety of life.

Since then, scientists have found out a lot more about the history of life — although there are still lots of missing pieces to the puzzle. And in the meantime … life goes on.

Glossary

When you see a word here in CAPITAL LETTERS LIKE THIS, it means that this word has a separate entry of its own where you can find more information.

CELLS A cell is a single unit of life. All cells "breathe" in some way, take in food, get rid of waste, produce more of themselves and eventually die.

All living things are made of cells. Some are made of just one cell, but most are made of thousands or even billions. We have about 60 billion cells in us, for example. Most cells are too small to see without a microscope, but the biggest cells of all are the yolks of birds' eggs.

CONTINENTS The six biggest pieces of land: Africa, Antarctica, Australia, Eurasia (Europe and Asia), North America and South America.

ALGAE Range from tiny single cells to the seaweed called giant kelp, which grows up to 60 m (66 yd.) long. Many algae look like PLANTS, but most scientists put them into a different group (or kingdom) altogether. There are lots of different SPECIES, but they can all be divided into red, brown or green algae. Most live in water, but a few grow on land — such as the green powdery stuff that you sometimes see on the bark of trees.

AMPHIBIANS A group of BACKBONED ANIMALS, most of which live on land as well as in water. Today, amphibians include newts, frogs, toads and salamanders.

ANIMALS One of the five kingdoms into which scientists divide all life-forms.

The other kingdoms are: Plants, Fungi (mushrooms, molds and toadstools), Protoctists (ALGAE and some single-celled life-forms) and Bacteria.

ARTHROPODS One of the biggest groups of ANIMALS. Arthropods are invertebrates — they have no BACKBONES. They have jointed legs and are usually covered with a hard protective skin, like armor. They include crabs, spiders, scorpions and INSECTS.

BACKBONES ANIMALS with backbones are called vertebrates. FISH are thought to have been the first vertebrate animals. Most of the larger animals today are vertebrates, including us humans. (ANIMALS without backbones are called invertebrates. Jellyfish, ARTHROPODS and MOLLUSKS are invertebrates.)

CRUST The hard, rocky layer that covers the Earth and carries the land and the sea. The crust varies in thickness from about 40 km (24 mi.) under land to only 6 km (3½ mi.) under the sea.

The crust is broken up into huge pieces, called plates. Underneath the crust there is a much thicker layer of hot, partially melted rock called the mantle.

Sometimes some of the melted rock in the mantle squeezes up through cracks in the ocean floor where one plate meets another. Then the rock cools down and hardens. And as it hardens, it forces the plates a little further apart, making them move a few centimeters (inches) each year.

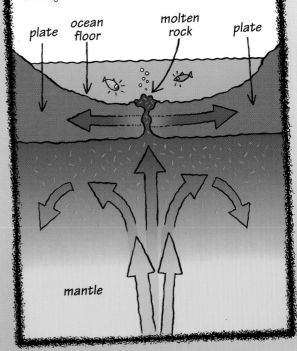

plate   ocean floor   molten rock   plate

mantle

FISH A group of ANIMALS that live in water and have BACKBONES, GILLS and fins. There are only two types of jawless fish today (lampreys and hagfish), all the others are jawed. Most jawed fish have bony skeletons (like goldfish and salmon), although a few have skeletons of cartilage (for example, sharks and rays).

GILLS The body part that many water ANIMALS use for breathing. The animal gulps in water through its mouth and then pushes it out through its gills. Water contains oxygen. As the water flows over the gills, they soak up the oxygen and send it to the bloodstream.

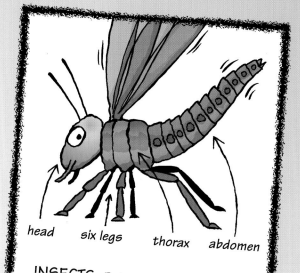

head   six legs   thorax   abdomen

INSECTS Belong to the enormous group of ANIMALS known as ARTHROPODS. The insect group itself is huge and includes flies, beetles, butterflies, dragonflies, termites, ants and wasps.
    All insects have three body parts (head, thorax, abdomen) and six legs.

LUNGS The part of the body that many land ANIMALS use for breathing oxygen from air.

MASS EXTINCTIONS Periods in Earth's history when large numbers of life-forms die out at about the same time. No one really knows what causes them, although they are usually linked to changes in the Earth's climate. So far, every mass extinction has been followed by an explosion of new life-forms.

octopus

MOLLUSKS A group of soft-bodied ANIMALS, without BACKBONES, that usually have some kind of shell. Mollusks include mussels, clams, oysters and snails, but also slugs, octopuses and squid.

MOSSES AND LIVERWORTS Very simple PLANTS that have no real roots or tubes for carrying food and water around inside them. Instead, food and water pass from cell to cell, like blotting paper soaks up ink.
    Although they are land plants, they usually only grow in damp, watery places.

PLANTS Like ANIMALS, plants make up one of the five kingdoms into which all life-forms are divided. Plants include MOSSES, ferns, conifers and flowering plants.

PREY Any animal that is killed and eaten as food by something else.

REPTILES A group of BACKBONED ANIMALS that today includes lizards, crocodiles, turtles, tortoises and snakes. Reptiles usually have a waterproof skin and lay eggs with tough, leathery shells. Some reptiles live on land and some live in the water, but they all lay their eggs on land.

SPECIES A group of ANIMALS of the same kind. They look similar and they can breed together to produce young. A barn owl is one species of bird, for example, and a parrot is a different species.

Index

Now read on. Don't miss VOLUME 3: THE DAY OF THE DINOSAURS The rise and fall of the world's greatest reptiles!

Name _____

Write the products.

a. $2 \times 3 =$ _____ $4 \times 2 =$ _____ $2 \times 7 =$ _____

b. $8 \times 2 =$ _____ $2 \times 4 =$ _____ $5 \times 2 =$ _____

c. $7 \times 2 =$ _____ $2 \times 8 =$ _____ $2 \times 5 =$ _____

d. $1 \times 2 =$ _____ $2 \times 2 =$ _____ $9 \times 2 =$ _____

e. $0 \times 2 =$ _____ $2 \times 7 =$ _____ $8 \times 2 =$ _____

f. $3 \times 2 =$ _____ $2 \times 6 =$ _____ $2 \times 0 =$ _____

g. $\begin{array}{r} 2 \\ \times 9 \\ \hline \end{array}$ $\begin{array}{r} 4 \\ \times 2 \\ \hline \end{array}$ $\begin{array}{r} 2 \\ \times 5 \\ \hline \end{array}$

h. $\begin{array}{r} 2 \\ \times 0 \\ \hline \end{array}$ $\begin{array}{r} 2 \\ \times 7 \\ \hline \end{array}$ $\begin{array}{r} 2 \\ \times 4 \\ \hline \end{array}$

i. $\begin{array}{r} 5 \\ \times 2 \\ \hline \end{array}$ $\begin{array}{r} 2 \\ \times 3 \\ \hline \end{array}$ $\begin{array}{r} 7 \\ \times 2 \\ \hline \end{array}$

j. $\begin{array}{r} 1 \\ \times 2 \\ \hline \end{array}$ $\begin{array}{r} 9 \\ \times 2 \\ \hline \end{array}$ $\begin{array}{r} 2 \\ \times 6 \\ \hline \end{array}$

k. $\begin{array}{r} 6 \\ \times 2 \\ \hline \end{array}$ $\begin{array}{r} 2 \\ \times 2 \\ \hline \end{array}$ $\begin{array}{r} 2 \\ \times 8 \\ \hline \end{array}$

l. $\begin{array}{r} 0 \\ \times 2 \\ \hline \end{array}$ $\begin{array}{r} 8 \\ \times 2 \\ \hline \end{array}$ $\begin{array}{r} 3 \\ \times 2 \\ \hline \end{array}$

Write the products.

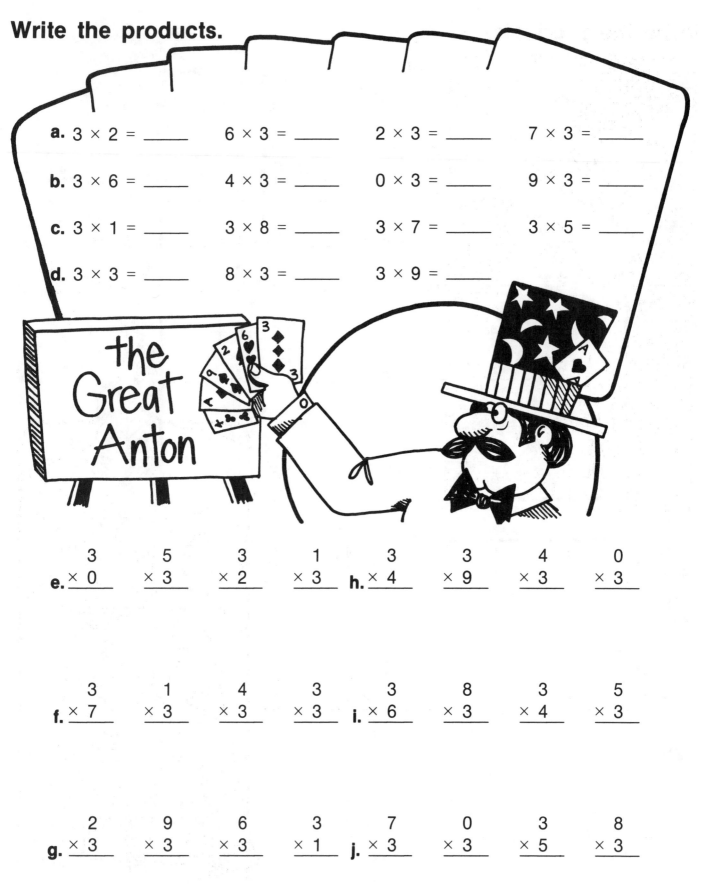

a. 3 × 2 = _____   6 × 3 = _____   2 × 3 = _____   7 × 3 = _____

b. 3 × 6 = _____   4 × 3 = _____   0 × 3 = _____   9 × 3 = _____

c. 3 × 1 = _____   3 × 8 = _____   3 × 7 = _____   3 × 5 = _____

d. 3 × 3 = _____   8 × 3 = _____   3 × 9 = _____

the
Great
Anton

e.
$$\begin{array}{r} 3 \\ \times\, 0 \\ \hline \end{array}\quad \begin{array}{r} 5 \\ \times\, 3 \\ \hline \end{array}\quad \begin{array}{r} 3 \\ \times\, 2 \\ \hline \end{array}\quad \begin{array}{r} 1 \\ \times\, 3 \\ \hline \end{array}\quad \textbf{h.}\begin{array}{r} 3 \\ \times\, 4 \\ \hline \end{array}\quad \begin{array}{r} 3 \\ \times\, 9 \\ \hline \end{array}\quad \begin{array}{r} 4 \\ \times\, 3 \\ \hline \end{array}\quad \begin{array}{r} 0 \\ \times\, 3 \\ \hline \end{array}$$

f.
$$\begin{array}{r} 3 \\ \times\, 7 \\ \hline \end{array}\quad \begin{array}{r} 1 \\ \times\, 3 \\ \hline \end{array}\quad \begin{array}{r} 4 \\ \times\, 3 \\ \hline \end{array}\quad \begin{array}{r} 3 \\ \times\, 3 \\ \hline \end{array}\quad \textbf{i.}\begin{array}{r} 3 \\ \times\, 6 \\ \hline \end{array}\quad \begin{array}{r} 8 \\ \times\, 3 \\ \hline \end{array}\quad \begin{array}{r} 3 \\ \times\, 4 \\ \hline \end{array}\quad \begin{array}{r} 5 \\ \times\, 3 \\ \hline \end{array}$$

g.
$$\begin{array}{r} 2 \\ \times\, 3 \\ \hline \end{array}\quad \begin{array}{r} 9 \\ \times\, 3 \\ \hline \end{array}\quad \begin{array}{r} 6 \\ \times\, 3 \\ \hline \end{array}\quad \begin{array}{r} 3 \\ \times\, 1 \\ \hline \end{array}\quad \textbf{j.}\begin{array}{r} 7 \\ \times\, 3 \\ \hline \end{array}\quad \begin{array}{r} 0 \\ \times\, 3 \\ \hline \end{array}\quad \begin{array}{r} 3 \\ \times\, 5 \\ \hline \end{array}\quad \begin{array}{r} 8 \\ \times\, 3 \\ \hline \end{array}$$

Write the products.

a. $6 \times 4 =$ _____ $4 \times 3 =$ _____ $0 \times 4 =$ _____

b. $4 \times 4 =$ _____ $4 \times 2 =$ _____ $7 \times 4 =$ _____

c. $4 \times 5 =$ _____ $4 \times 9 =$ _____ $4 \times 8 =$ _____

d. $5 \times 4 =$ _____ $9 \times 4 =$ _____ $8 \times 4 =$ _____

e. $9 \times 4 =$ _____ $4 \times 0 =$ _____ $4 \times 6 =$ _____

f. $3 \times 4 =$ _____ $1 \times 4 =$ _____ $4 \times 9 =$ _____

g. $4 \times 0 =$ _____ $9 \times 4 =$ _____

h.
$$\begin{array}{cc} 4 \\ \times\,6 \\ \hline \end{array} \quad \begin{array}{cc} 0 \\ \times\,4 \\ \hline \end{array} \quad \begin{array}{cc} 3 \\ \times\,4 \\ \hline \end{array} \quad \begin{array}{cc} 4 \\ \times\,8 \\ \hline \end{array} \quad \begin{array}{cc} 9 \\ \times\,4 \\ \hline \end{array} \quad \begin{array}{cc} 2 \\ \times\,4 \\ \hline \end{array}$$

i.
$$\begin{array}{cc} 1 \\ \times\,4 \\ \hline \end{array} \quad \begin{array}{cc} 5 \\ \times\,4 \\ \hline \end{array} \quad \begin{array}{cc} 6 \\ \times\,4 \\ \hline \end{array} \quad \begin{array}{cc} 7 \\ \times\,4 \\ \hline \end{array} \quad \begin{array}{cc} 4 \\ \times\,4 \\ \hline \end{array} \quad \begin{array}{cc} 4 \\ \times\,3 \\ \hline \end{array}$$

j.
$$\begin{array}{cc} 4 \\ \times\,1 \\ \hline \end{array} \quad \begin{array}{cc} 4 \\ \times\,0 \\ \hline \end{array} \quad \begin{array}{cc} 4 \\ \times\,9 \\ \hline \end{array} \quad \begin{array}{cc} 8 \\ \times\,4 \\ \hline \end{array} \quad \begin{array}{cc} 4 \\ \times\,7 \\ \hline \end{array} \quad \begin{array}{cc} 4 \\ \times\,5 \\ \hline \end{array}$$

Poof!

Name _____

Write the products.

	a.	b.	c.	d.
	5 × 2 = _____	4 × 5 = _____	5 × 7 = _____	8 × 5 = _____
	5 × 0 = _____	2 × 5 = _____	5 × 4 = _____	6 × 5 = _____
	9 × 5 = _____	5 × 1 = _____	7 × 5 = _____	5 × 5 = _____
	6 × 5 = _____	5 × 3 = _____	0 × 5 = _____	5 × 6 = _____
	5 × 9 = _____	1 × 5 = _____	5 × 8 = _____	3 × 5 = _____

e.
$\begin{array}{r} 5 \\ \times 3 \\ \hline \end{array}$
$\begin{array}{r} 0 \\ \times 5 \\ \hline \end{array}$
$\begin{array}{r} 4 \\ \times 5 \\ \hline \end{array}$
$\begin{array}{r} 5 \\ \times 8 \\ \hline \end{array}$
h.
$\begin{array}{r} 6 \\ \times 5 \\ \hline \end{array}$
$\begin{array}{r} 5 \\ \times 5 \\ \hline \end{array}$
$\begin{array}{r} 1 \\ \times 5 \\ \hline \end{array}$
$\begin{array}{r} 5 \\ \times 9 \\ \hline \end{array}$

f.
$\begin{array}{r} 7 \\ \times 5 \\ \hline \end{array}$
$\begin{array}{r} 5 \\ \times 2 \\ \hline \end{array}$
$\begin{array}{r} 5 \\ \times 6 \\ \hline \end{array}$
$\begin{array}{r} 9 \\ \times 5 \\ \hline \end{array}$
i.
$\begin{array}{r} 5 \\ \times 6 \\ \hline \end{array}$
$\begin{array}{r} 8 \\ \times 5 \\ \hline \end{array}$
$\begin{array}{r} 5 \\ \times 5 \\ \hline \end{array}$
$\begin{array}{r} 5 \\ \times 7 \\ \hline \end{array}$

g.
$\begin{array}{r} 5 \\ \times 0 \\ \hline \end{array}$
$\begin{array}{r} 3 \\ \times 5 \\ \hline \end{array}$
$\begin{array}{r} 5 \\ \times 1 \\ \hline \end{array}$
$\begin{array}{r} 6 \\ \times 5 \\ \hline \end{array}$
j.
$\begin{array}{r} 5 \\ \times 3 \\ \hline \end{array}$
$\begin{array}{r} 5 \\ \times 4 \\ \hline \end{array}$
$\begin{array}{r} 5 \\ \times 9 \\ \hline \end{array}$
$\begin{array}{r} 8 \\ \times 5 \\ \hline \end{array}$

Write the products.

a. $6 \times 2 =$ _____ $4 \times 6 =$ _____ $7 \times 6 =$ _____

b. $1 \times 6 =$ _____ $6 \times 5 =$ _____ $9 \times 6 =$ _____

c. $3 \times 6 =$ _____ $6 \times 6 =$ _____ $6 \times 1 =$ _____

d. $6 \times 7 =$ _____ $5 \times 6 =$ _____ $6 \times 9 =$ _____

e. $0 \times 6 =$ _____ $6 \times 3 =$ _____ $6 \times 4 =$ _____

MATCHES

f.

$$\begin{array}{r} 6 \\ \times\,6 \\ \hline \end{array} \quad \begin{array}{r} 5 \\ \times\,6 \\ \hline \end{array} \quad \begin{array}{r} 7 \\ \times\,6 \\ \hline \end{array} \quad \begin{array}{r} 6 \\ \times\,0 \\ \hline \end{array} \quad \begin{array}{r} 2 \\ \times\,6 \\ \hline \end{array} \quad \begin{array}{r} 6 \\ \times\,8 \\ \hline \end{array}$$

g.

$$\begin{array}{r} 6 \\ \times\,3 \\ \hline \end{array} \quad \begin{array}{r} 6 \\ \times\,2 \\ \hline \end{array} \quad \begin{array}{r} 6 \\ \times\,4 \\ \hline \end{array} \quad \begin{array}{r} 9 \\ \times\,6 \\ \hline \end{array} \quad \begin{array}{r} 1 \\ \times\,6 \\ \hline \end{array}$$

Poof!

h.

$$\begin{array}{r} 8 \\ \times\,6 \\ \hline \end{array} \quad \begin{array}{r} 4 \\ \times\,6 \\ \hline \end{array} \quad \begin{array}{r} 6 \\ \times\,1 \\ \hline \end{array} \quad \begin{array}{r} 3 \\ \times\,6 \\ \hline \end{array} \quad \begin{array}{r} 6 \\ \times\,9 \\ \hline \end{array} \qquad\qquad \begin{array}{r} 6 \\ \times\,7 \\ \hline \end{array}$$

Write the products.

a. 2 × 7 = _____

b. 7 × 2 = _____   6 × 7 = _____

c. 7 × 7 = _____   3 × 7 = _____

d. 5 × 7 = _____

e. 7 × 9 = _____

f. 0 × 7 = _____

g. 1 × 7 = _____

h. 8 × 7 = _____

i. 7 × 5 = _____   4 × 7 = _____

j. 7 × 8 = _____   9 × 7 = _____

k.
$$\begin{array}{r} 7 \\ \times\ 5 \\ \hline \end{array} \qquad \begin{array}{r} 0 \\ \times\ 7 \\ \hline \end{array} \qquad \begin{array}{r} 7 \\ \times\ 4 \\ \hline \end{array}$$

l.
$$\begin{array}{r} 7 \\ \times\ 0 \\ \hline \end{array} \qquad \begin{array}{r} 7 \\ \times\ 6 \\ \hline \end{array} \qquad \begin{array}{r} 2 \\ \times\ 7 \\ \hline \end{array}$$

m.
$$\begin{array}{r} 7 \\ \times\ 8 \\ \hline \end{array} \qquad \begin{array}{r} 9 \\ \times\ 7 \\ \hline \end{array} \qquad \begin{array}{r} 7 \\ \times\ 1 \\ \hline \end{array}$$

n.
$$\begin{array}{r} 7 \\ \times\ 4 \\ \hline \end{array} \qquad \begin{array}{r} 3 \\ \times\ 7 \\ \hline \end{array} \qquad \begin{array}{r} 8 \\ \times\ 7 \\ \hline \end{array}$$

o.
$$\begin{array}{r} 7 \\ \times\ 9 \\ \hline \end{array} \qquad \begin{array}{r} 4 \\ \times\ 7 \\ \hline \end{array} \qquad \begin{array}{r} 7 \\ \times\ 2 \\ \hline \end{array}$$

p.
$$\begin{array}{r} 7 \\ \times\ 7 \\ \hline \end{array} \qquad \begin{array}{r} 6 \\ \times\ 7 \\ \hline \end{array} \qquad \begin{array}{r} 5 \\ \times\ 7 \\ \hline \end{array}$$

FS-2673   Math Workbook-Multiplication & Division

Write the products.

a.	b.	c.	d.	e.	f.
$\begin{array}{r} 8 \\ \times\, 2 \\ \hline \end{array}$	$\begin{array}{r} 4 \\ \times\, 8 \\ \hline \end{array}$	$\begin{array}{r} 8 \\ \times\, 6 \\ \hline \end{array}$	$\begin{array}{r} 7 \\ \times\, 8 \\ \hline \end{array}$	$\begin{array}{r} 8 \\ \times\, 8 \\ \hline \end{array}$	$\begin{array}{r} 9 \\ \times\, 8 \\ \hline \end{array}$
$\begin{array}{r} 8 \\ \times\, 0 \\ \hline \end{array}$	$\begin{array}{r} 2 \\ \times\, 8 \\ \hline \end{array}$	$\begin{array}{r} 8 \\ \times\, 9 \\ \hline \end{array}$	$\begin{array}{r} 6 \\ \times\, 8 \\ \hline \end{array}$	$\begin{array}{r} 3 \\ \times\, 8 \\ \hline \end{array}$	
$\begin{array}{r} 8 \\ \times\, 7 \\ \hline \end{array}$	$\begin{array}{r} 0 \\ \times\, 8 \\ \hline \end{array}$	$\begin{array}{r} 8 \\ \times\, 4 \\ \hline \end{array}$	$\begin{array}{r} 1 \\ \times\, 8 \\ \hline \end{array}$	$\begin{array}{r} 8 \\ \times\, 5 \\ \hline \end{array}$	$\begin{array}{r} 8 \\ \times\, 8 \\ \hline \end{array}$

g.	h.	i.
$3 \times 8 = \underline{\hspace{1cm}}$	$8 \times 6 = \underline{\hspace{1cm}}$	$8 \times 5 = \underline{\hspace{1cm}}$
$4 \times 8 = \underline{\hspace{1cm}}$	$8 \times 2 = \underline{\hspace{1cm}}$	$6 \times 8 = \underline{\hspace{1cm}}$
$8 \times 0 = \underline{\hspace{1cm}}$	$7 \times 8 = \underline{\hspace{1cm}}$	$8 \times 9 = \underline{\hspace{1cm}}$
$8 \times 4 = \underline{\hspace{1cm}}$	$8 \times 1 = \underline{\hspace{1cm}}$	$8 \times 7 = \underline{\hspace{1cm}}$

Write the products.

a. 9 × 4 = _____   7 × 9 = _____

b. 9 × 8 = _____   3 × 9 = _____

c. 0 × 9 = _____   6 × 9 = _____

d. 9 × 6 = _____

e. 2 × 9 = _____

f. 9 × 5 = _____

g. 1 × 9 = _____

h. 9 × 7 = _____

i. 9 × 0 = _____

j. 9 × 3 = _____   4 × 9 = _____

k. 5 × 9 = _____   9 × 1 = _____

l. 9 × 9 = _____   9 × 6 = _____

m.
$$\begin{array}{r} 9 \\ \times\ 0 \\ \hline \end{array} \qquad \begin{array}{r} 3 \\ \times\ 9 \\ \hline \end{array} \qquad \begin{array}{r} 7 \\ \times\ 9 \\ \hline \end{array} \qquad \begin{array}{r} 9 \\ \times\ 6 \\ \hline \end{array}$$

n.
$$\begin{array}{r} 9 \\ \times\ 8 \\ \hline \end{array} \qquad \begin{array}{r} 9 \\ \times\ 2 \\ \hline \end{array} \qquad \begin{array}{r} 8 \\ \times\ 9 \\ \hline \end{array} \qquad \begin{array}{r} 9 \\ \times\ 9 \\ \hline \end{array}$$

o.
$$\begin{array}{r} 9 \\ \times\ 5 \\ \hline \end{array} \qquad \begin{array}{r} 4 \\ \times\ 9 \\ \hline \end{array} \qquad \begin{array}{r} 0 \\ \times\ 9 \\ \hline \end{array} \qquad \begin{array}{r} 9 \\ \times\ 4 \\ \hline \end{array}$$

p.
$$\begin{array}{r} 9 \\ \times\ 7 \\ \hline \end{array} \qquad \begin{array}{r} 6 \\ \times\ 9 \\ \hline \end{array} \qquad \begin{array}{r} 1 \\ \times\ 9 \\ \hline \end{array} \qquad \begin{array}{r} 9 \\ \times\ 3 \\ \hline \end{array}$$

q.
$$\begin{array}{r} 2 \\ \times\ 9 \\ \hline \end{array} \qquad \begin{array}{r} 5 \\ \times\ 9 \\ \hline \end{array} \qquad \begin{array}{r} 7 \\ \times\ 9 \\ \hline \end{array} \qquad \begin{array}{r} 3 \\ \times\ 9 \\ \hline \end{array}$$

r.
$$\begin{array}{r} 8 \\ \times\ 9 \\ \hline \end{array} \qquad \begin{array}{r} 9 \\ \times\ 0 \\ \hline \end{array} \qquad \begin{array}{r} 9 \\ \times\ 9 \\ \hline \end{array} \qquad \begin{array}{r} 9 \\ \times\ 6 \\ \hline \end{array}$$

FS-2673   Math Workbook-Multiplication & Division

Circle the correct answer.

a. 8 × 4 =	36	(32)	**d.** 6 × 8 =	40	48	**g.** 7 × 6 =	42	45

a. 8 × 4 = | 36 (32)
2 × 2 = | 6   4
6 × 9 = | 54   56
5 × 7 = | 32   35
7 × 9 = | 63   52
9 × 8 = | 56   72

b. 6 × 2 = | 10   12
3 × 9 = | 27   28
7 × 9 = | 25   63
4 × 3 = | 12   15
7 × 2 = | 14   20
5 × 4 = | 20   25

c. 6 × 3 = | 12   18
7 × 5 = | 35   24
2 × 8 = | 16   24
9 × 2 = | 18   20
8 × 5 = | 25   40
7 × 7 = | 49   48

d. 6 × 8 = | 40   48
8 × 3 = | 24   36
4 × 2 = | 8   10
3 × 2 = | 6   8
6 × 8 = | 48   54
2 × 9 = | 14   18

e. 7 × 3 = | 20   21
9 × 1 = | 0   9
4 × 7 = | 28   21
8 × 8 = | 64   32
5 × 9 = | 25   45
9 × 7 = | 56   63

f. 8 × 1 = | 0   8
5 × 5 = | 24   25
0 × 6 = | 0   6
5 × 3 = | 15   10
8 × 9 = | 64   72
7 × 4 = | 14   28

g. 7 × 6 = | 42   45
4 × 8 = | 24   32
9 × 3 = | 27   30
6 × 4 = | 20   24
8 × 6 = | 40   48
5 × 8 = | 40   45

h. 7 × 0 = | 0   14
6 × 6 = | 32   36
3 × 7 = | 21   25
7 × 8 = | 35   56
5 × 6 = | 20   30
7 × 2 = | 14   18

i. 9 × 5 = | 45   48
3 × 8 = | 20   24
9 × 6 = | 54   35
8 × 2 = | 10   16
4 × 4 = | 16   18
8 × 7 = | 50   56

FS-2673   Math Workbook-Multiplication & Division

Write the products.

a. $2 \times 3 =$ _____ $6 \times 7 =$ _____ $3 \times 9 =$ _____

b. $7 \times 2 =$ _____ $3 \times 6 =$ _____ $4 \times 3 =$ _____

c. $9 \times 4 =$ _____ $8 \times 1 =$ _____ $4 \times 7 =$ _____

d. $6 \times 5 =$ _____ $9 \times 8 =$ _____ $7 \times 7 =$ _____

e. $8 \times 8 =$ _____ $5 \times 7 =$ _____ $2 \times 9 =$ _____

f. $8 \times 6 =$ _____ $0 \times 7 =$ _____ $8 \times 7 =$ _____

g. $\begin{array}{r} 7 \\ \times 6 \\ \hline \end{array}$ $\begin{array}{r} 0 \\ \times 8 \\ \hline \end{array}$ $\begin{array}{r} 9 \\ \times 2 \\ \hline \end{array}$ **j.** $\begin{array}{r} 4 \\ \times 5 \\ \hline \end{array}$ $\begin{array}{r} 7 \\ \times 9 \\ \hline \end{array}$ $\begin{array}{r} 4 \\ \times 6 \\ \hline \end{array}$

h. $\begin{array}{r} 5 \\ \times 5 \\ \hline \end{array}$ $\begin{array}{r} 8 \\ \times 3 \\ \hline \end{array}$ $\begin{array}{r} 2 \\ \times 6 \\ \hline \end{array}$ **k.** $\begin{array}{r} 3 \\ \times 5 \\ \hline \end{array}$ $\begin{array}{r} 6 \\ \times 6 \\ \hline \end{array}$ $\begin{array}{r} 8 \\ \times 9 \\ \hline \end{array}$

i. $\begin{array}{r} 9 \\ \times 6 \\ \hline \end{array}$ $\begin{array}{r} 5 \\ \times 8 \\ \hline \end{array}$ $\begin{array}{r} 3 \\ \times 7 \\ \hline \end{array}$ **l.** $\begin{array}{r} 9 \\ \times 9 \\ \hline \end{array}$ $\begin{array}{r} 8 \\ \times 4 \\ \hline \end{array}$ $\begin{array}{r} 3 \\ \times 3 \\ \hline \end{array}$

Write the number sentence and label your answer.

a. There are 3 spiders. If each spider has 8 legs, how many legs are there in all?

_____

There are _____ _____ .

b. If there are 5 ants, each with 6 legs, how many legs are there?

_____

There are _____ _____ .

c. An octopus has 8 arms. How many arms would there be if you had 4 octopuses?

_____

There would be _____ _____ .

d. If one cricket has 6 legs, how many legs would 3 crickets have all together?

_____

There would be _____ _____ .

e. There are 3 dogs. If each dog has 4 legs, how many legs are there all together?

_____

There are _____ _____ .

f. Ducks have 2 feet. If there are 7 ducks, how many feet are there in all?

_____

There are _____ _____ .

g. Snakes don't have legs. If there are 3 snakes, how many legs are there?

_____

There are _____ _____ .

Write the number sentence and label your answer.

d. A football team gets 6 points for a touchdown. How many points would 8 touchdowns be?

_____

It would be _____ _____ .

a. Baseball games have 9 innings. If each inning has 3 outs, how many outs are there in a game?

_____

There are _____ _____ .

e. If you swam 8 laps a day for 7 days, how many laps would you swim all together?

_____

That would be _____ _____ .

b. There are 4 people at each Ping-Pong table. If there are 9 tables, how many people are playing?

_____

There are _____ _____ .

f. Dad jogs 6 miles a day. How many miles would he jog in 4 days?

_____

Dad would jog _____ _____ .

c. There are 5 players on a basketball team. If they each score 9 points, what would the team's score be?

_____

The score would be _____ .

g. In tennis, you play 6 games each set. If you play 7 sets, how many games would you play?

_____

You would play _____ _____ .

Remember to **add** what you **carry**!

?

I call it regrouping!

Find the products.

a.
```
  23        37        95
×  3      ×  4      ×  2
```

b.
```
  38        86        27        49        65        18
×  2      ×  5      ×  3    f.× 2      ×  4      ×  5
```

c.
```
  46        20        49        52        93        72
×  3      ×  4      ×  2    g.× 7      ×  8      ×  6
```

d.
```
  19        38        64        42        80        24
×  7      ×  8      ×  6    h.× 9      ×  5      ×  7
```

e.
```
  48        15        36        57        19        60
×  7      ×  9      ×  8    i.× 7      ×  9      ×  7
```

Find the products.

a.	415 × 3	987 × 2	328 × 5	238 × 4	156 × 3
b.	864 × 5	276 × 4	529 × 3	190 × 2	209 × 4
c.	748 × 5	486 × 3	507 × 4	359 × 5	908 × 2
d.	550 × 7	517 × 6	128 × 9	463 × 8	418 × 7
e.	944 × 9	308 × 7	291 × 8	674 × 6	890 × 9
f.	327 × 8	876 × 9	909 × 6	463 × 7	608 × 8

Example:

$$
\begin{array}{r}
46 \\
\times\ 36 \\
\hline
276 \\
+\ 1380 \\
\hline
1656
\end{array}
$$

You're in BIG trouble if you don't start your SECOND product with a ZERO!

Add the two products, and you're home free!

Multiply. Then add the products.

a.
$\begin{array}{r} 25 \\ \times\ 48 \\ \hline \end{array}$
$\begin{array}{r} 47 \\ \times\ 56 \\ \hline \end{array}$
$\begin{array}{r} 83 \\ \times\ 34 \\ \hline \end{array}$
$\begin{array}{r} 36 \\ \times\ 92 \\ \hline \end{array}$

b.
$\begin{array}{r} 42 \\ \times\ 49 \\ \hline \end{array}$
$\begin{array}{r} 50 \\ \times\ 87 \\ \hline \end{array}$
$\begin{array}{r} 71 \\ \times\ 58 \\ \hline \end{array}$
$\begin{array}{r} 63 \\ \times\ 79 \\ \hline \end{array}$
$\begin{array}{r} 38 \\ \times\ 29 \\ \hline \end{array}$

c.
$\begin{array}{r} 56 \\ \times\ 33 \\ \hline \end{array}$
$\begin{array}{r} 84 \\ \times\ 25 \\ \hline \end{array}$
$\begin{array}{r} 27 \\ \times\ 54 \\ \hline \end{array}$
$\begin{array}{r} 93 \\ \times\ 26 \\ \hline \end{array}$
$\begin{array}{r} 78 \\ \times\ 57 \\ \hline \end{array}$

d.
$\begin{array}{r} 45 \\ \times\ 37 \\ \hline \end{array}$
$\begin{array}{r} 67 \\ \times\ 88 \\ \hline \end{array}$
$\begin{array}{r} 72 \\ \times\ 39 \\ \hline \end{array}$
$\begin{array}{r} 83 \\ \times\ 50 \\ \hline \end{array}$
$\begin{array}{r} 46 \\ \times\ 74 \\ \hline \end{array}$

Name _____

A sad case of Digit Disease.

$$\begin{array}{r} 345 \\ \times\ 37 \\ \hline 2415 \\ 1035 \\ \hline 3440 \end{array}$$

I've been cured!! Now it's a breeze!

$$\begin{array}{r} 345 \\ \times\ 37 \\ \hline 2415 \\ 10350 \\ \hline 12765 \end{array}$$

Multiply. Then add the products.

a.
$$\begin{array}{r} 674 \\ \times\ 27 \\ \hline \end{array}$$
$$\begin{array}{r} 450 \\ \times\ 65 \\ \hline \end{array}$$
$$\begin{array}{r} 917 \\ \times\ 25 \\ \hline \end{array}$$
$$\begin{array}{r} 542 \\ \times\ 73 \\ \hline \end{array}$$
$$\begin{array}{r} 406 \\ \times\ 26 \\ \hline \end{array}$$

b.
$$\begin{array}{r} 853 \\ \times\ 74 \\ \hline \end{array}$$
$$\begin{array}{r} 346 \\ \times\ 54 \\ \hline \end{array}$$
$$\begin{array}{r} 902 \\ \times\ 48 \\ \hline \end{array}$$
$$\begin{array}{r} 300 \\ \times\ 46 \\ \hline \end{array}$$
$$\begin{array}{r} 761 \\ \times\ 25 \\ \hline \end{array}$$

c.
$$\begin{array}{r} 674 \\ \times\ 27 \\ \hline \end{array}$$
$$\begin{array}{r} 808 \\ \times\ 34 \\ \hline \end{array}$$
$$\begin{array}{r} 432 \\ \times\ 59 \\ \hline \end{array}$$
$$\begin{array}{r} 735 \\ \times\ 74 \\ \hline \end{array}$$
$$\begin{array}{r} 207 \\ \times\ 98 \\ \hline \end{array}$$

d.
$$\begin{array}{r} 327 \\ \times\ 58 \\ \hline \end{array}$$
$$\begin{array}{r} 772 \\ \times\ 48 \\ \hline \end{array}$$
$$\begin{array}{r} 307 \\ \times\ 59 \\ \hline \end{array}$$
$$\begin{array}{r} 912 \\ \times\ 79 \\ \hline \end{array}$$
$$\begin{array}{r} 686 \\ \times\ 68 \\ \hline \end{array}$$

Millie's Movers charge $9 per hour.
Fill out a bill for each customer.

a. Bill for five hours

c. Bill for seven hours

e. Bill for nine hours

b. Bill for eight hours

d. Bill for six hours

f. Bill for four hours

Jack makes handmade rings and charges $7 each.
Figure out how much to charge each customer.

g. I'll buy four. BILL

h. I'll buy eight. BILL

i. I'll buy nine. BILL

j. BILL I'll buy six.

k. BILL I'll buy five.

Sam is a vet. He charges $8 for each pet he sees. Figure out how much money he made each day.

l. MON	m. TUES	n. WED	o. THURS	p. FRI	q. SAT
He saw six pets.	He saw nine pets.	He saw seven pets.	He saw four pets.	He saw eight pets.	He saw no pets.

TOY SHOP

Cars — 59 cents each

Baseballs — 78 cents each

Stuffed Animals — 37 cents each

Figure out each bill. Show the problem as well as the answer. Good luck!

a. Five cars

d. Four baseballs

g. Six stuffed animals

b. Two stuffed animals

e. Two cars

h. Two baseballs

c. Three cars

f. Nine stuffed animals

i. Six baseballs

Name _____

Write the quotients.

a. 12 ÷ 6 = _____   10 ÷ 2 = _____   16 ÷ 2 = _____

b. 8 ÷ 4 = _____   2 ÷ 2 = _____   4 ÷ 2 = _____

c. 18 ÷ 2 = _____   2 ÷ 1 = _____   10 ÷ 2 = _____

d. 16 ÷ 8 = _____   12 ÷ 2 = _____   14 ÷ 7 = _____

e. 2 ÷ 1 = _____   6 ÷ 2 = _____   10 ÷ 2 = _____

f. 8 ÷ 2 = _____   18 ÷ 9 = _____   6 ÷ 3 = _____

g. 14 ÷ 7 = _____   8 ÷ 4 = _____   18 ÷ 2 = _____

h. 2 ÷ 2 = _____   12 ÷ 6 = _____   6 ÷ 2 = _____

i. 2) 12   2) 4   4) 8   9) 18   7) 14

j. 2) 16   1) 2   2) 6   4) 8

k. 3) 6   9) 18   2) 10   2) 2

l. 2) 18   6) 12   2) 8   5) 10

Write the quotients.

a. 27 ÷ 3 = _____   24 ÷ 8 = _____   21 ÷ 7 = _____

b. 24 ÷ 3 = _____   15 ÷ 5 = _____   12 ÷ 4 = _____

c. 15 ÷ 3 = _____   27 ÷ 9 = _____   9 ÷ 3 = _____

d. 18 ÷ 6 = _____   21 ÷ 3 = _____   6 ÷ 2 = _____

e. 12 ÷ 3 = _____   6 ÷ 3 = _____   18 ÷ 3 = _____

f. 3)‾12‾   3)‾9‾   3)‾27‾   1)‾3‾   3)‾18‾

g. 3)‾6‾   5)‾15‾   3)‾24‾   3)‾3‾   9)‾27‾

h. 3)‾21‾   8)‾24‾   7)‾21‾   3)‾9‾   4)‾12‾

Name _____

Write the quotients.

a.

24 ÷ 6 = _____   32 ÷ 4 = _____

b.

4 ÷ 1 = _____   8 ÷ 4 = _____

c.

28 ÷ 4 = _____   36 ÷ 4 = _____

d.

20 ÷ 4 = _____   32 ÷ 8 = _____

e.

24 ÷ 4 = _____   12 ÷ 3 = _____

f.

8 ÷ 2 = _____   16 ÷ 4 = _____

g.

36 ÷ 9 = _____   24 ÷ 4 = _____

h.

4 ÷ 4 = _____   28 ÷ 7 = _____

i. $4\overline{)8}$ $4\overline{)16}$ $9\overline{)36}$

j. $7\overline{)28}$ $1\overline{)4}$ $4\overline{)12}$

k. $4\overline{)36}$ $5\overline{)20}$ $4\overline{)16}$

l. $4\overline{)8}$ $4\overline{)32}$ $9\overline{)36}$

m. $8\overline{)32}$ $4\overline{)4}$ $4\overline{)28}$

FS-2673 Math Workbook-Multiplication & Division

Write the quotients.

a. 45 ÷ 5 = _____   35 ÷ 7 = _____   **f.** 30 ÷ 5 = _____   40 ÷ 8 = _____

b. 30 ÷ 6 = _____   10 ÷ 5 = _____   **g.** 45 ÷ 9 = _____   15 ÷ 3 = _____

c. 25 ÷ 5 = _____   40 ÷ 5 = _____   **h.** 5 ÷ 5 = _____   20 ÷ 5 = _____

d. 20 ÷ 4 = _____   15 ÷ 5 = _____   **i.** 35 ÷ 5 = _____   10 ÷ 2 = _____

e. 15 ÷ 5 = _____   45 ÷ 9 = _____   **j.** 5 ÷ 1 = _____   30 ÷ 6 = _____

k. $9\overline{)45}$ $5\overline{)20}$ $5\overline{)35}$ **n.** $5\overline{)10}$ $4\overline{)20}$ $6\overline{)30}$

l. $5\overline{)45}$ $1\overline{)5}$ $7\overline{)35}$ **o.** $5\overline{)25}$ $5\overline{)5}$ $5\overline{)40}$

m. $5\overline{)30}$ $8\overline{)40}$ $3\overline{)15}$ **p.** $1\overline{)5}$ $5\overline{)15}$ $5\overline{)45}$

Name _____

Write the quotients.

Abracadabra

a. 18 ÷ 6 = _____

b. 48 ÷ 8 = _____

c. 54 ÷ 6 = _____   36 ÷ 6 = _____   24 ÷ 6 = _____

d. 12 ÷ 6 = _____   6 ÷ 1 = _____   30 ÷ 5 = _____

e. 48 ÷ 6 = _____   54 ÷ 9 = _____   18 ÷ 3 = _____

f. 6 ÷ 6 = _____   48 ÷ 8 = _____   36 ÷ 6 = _____

g. 42 ÷ 6 = _____   12 ÷ 2 = _____   18 ÷ 6 = _____

h. $6\overline{)30}$ $1\overline{)6}$ $4\overline{)24}$ $6\overline{)24}$

i. $8\overline{)48}$ $5\overline{)30}$ $6\overline{)24}$ $6\overline{)12}$

j. $6\overline{)18}$ $6\overline{)36}$ $9\overline{)54}$ $6\overline{)48}$

k. $6\overline{)12}$ $6\overline{)30}$ $3\overline{)18}$ $2\overline{)12}$ $6\overline{)6}$ $7\overline{)42}$

l. $4\overline{)24}$ $6\overline{)54}$ $6\overline{)36}$ $6\overline{)24}$ $3\overline{)18}$ $6\overline{)12}$

Write the quotients.

a.

$7 \overline{)63}$ $\qquad$ $7 \overline{)49}$ $\qquad$ $7 \overline{)35}$

b.

$3 \overline{)21}$ $\qquad$ $7 \overline{)28}$ $\qquad$ $6 \overline{)42}$ $\qquad$ $7 \overline{)56}$

c.

$5 \overline{)35}$ $\qquad$ $2 \overline{)14}$ $\qquad$ $7 \overline{)14}$ $\qquad$ $7 \overline{)21}$

d.

$7 \overline{)7}$ $\qquad$ $9 \overline{)63}$ $\qquad$ $4 \overline{)28}$ $\qquad$ $7 \overline{)14}$

e. $63 \div 9 = $ _____ $7 \div 7 = $ _____ $42 \div 7 = $ _____ $56 \div 8 = $ _____

f. $28 \div 4 = $ _____ $7 \div 1 = $ _____ $63 \div 7 = $ _____ $49 \div 7 = $ _____

g. $42 \div 6 = $ _____ $35 \div 7 = $ _____ $28 \div 7 = $ _____ $21 \div 3 = $ _____

h. $14 \div 7 = $ _____ $56 \div 7 = $ _____ $35 \div 5 = $ _____ $28 \div 4 = $ _____

Name _____

Write the quotients.

a. $56 \div 7 =$ _____ $32 \div 8 =$ _____ $24 \div 3 =$ _____

b. $64 \div 8 =$ _____ $8 \div 8 =$ _____ $16 \div 2 =$ _____

c. $72 \div 9 =$ _____ $56 \div 8 =$ _____ $8 \div 1 =$ _____

d. $24 \div 8 =$ _____ $40 \div 5 =$ _____ $48 \div 8 =$ _____

e. $40 \div 8 =$ _____ $16 \div 8 =$ _____ $32 \div 4 =$ _____

f. $72 \div 8 =$ _____ $64 \div 8 =$ _____

g. $48 \div 6 =$ _____

h.
$8\overline{)\,64}$ $8\overline{)\,40}$ $3\overline{)\,24}$ $8\overline{)\,8}$ $8\overline{)\,24}$

i.
$5\overline{)\,40}$ $7\overline{)\,56}$ $8\overline{)\,32}$ $1\overline{)\,8}$ $8\overline{)\,72}$

j.
$4\overline{)\,32}$ $8\overline{)\,48}$ $2\overline{)\,16}$ $8\overline{)\,56}$ $8\overline{)\,64}$

k.
$6\overline{)\,48}$ $9\overline{)\,72}$ $8\overline{)\,16}$ $3\overline{)\,24}$ $5\overline{)\,40}$

Write the quotients.

a. 72 ÷ 9 = _____   45 ÷ 9 = _____   18 ÷ 9 = _____   81 ÷ 9 = _____

b. 27 ÷ 9 = _____   63 ÷ 7 = _____   36 ÷ 9 = _____   54 ÷ 6 = _____

c. 9 ÷ 9 = _____   72 ÷ 8 = _____   36 ÷ 4 = _____   63 ÷ 9 = _____

d. 54 ÷ 6 = _____   81 ÷ 9 = _____   54 ÷ 9 = _____   18 ÷ 9 = _____

e. 9 ÷ 1 = _____   63 ÷ 9 = _____   27 ÷ 3 = _____   45 ÷ 5 = _____

f. 4)36   2)18   9)9   6)54   9)81

g. 9)54   7)63   8)72   3)27   9)18

h. 6)54   9)36   9)81   9)45   8)72

i. 9)9   9)18   5)45   9)72   9)27

Write the quotients. Make a big X or an O to play tic-tac-toe.

c.

9)‾81	7)‾35	3)‾15
6)‾30	8)‾72	9)‾45
5)‾25	7)‾63	3)‾27

X = 5   O = 9   winner _____

a.

7)‾49	4)‾8	2)‾4
7)‾14	8)‾16	3)‾21
7)‾49	6)‾12	5)‾35

X = 2   O = 7   winner _____

d.

7)‾56	9)‾27	8)‾64
5)‾15	6)‾18	9)‾72
3)‾9	3)‾24	5)‾40

X = 3   O = 8   winner _____

b.

9)‾36	6)‾24	6)‾36
4)‾16	7)‾42	1)‾4
2)‾12	5)‾30	8)‾32

X = 4   O = 6   winner _____

e.

2)‾18	5)‾45	2)‾6
4)‾36	7)‾21	1)‾9
9)‾81	6)‾54	8)‾24

X = 9   O = 3   winner _____

Write the quotients.

a.

$16 \div 4 =$ _____ $10 \div 5 =$ _____ $4 \div 4 =$ _____ $21 \div 7 =$ _____

b.

$35 \div 7 =$ _____ $45 \div 9 =$ _____ $10 \div 2 =$ _____ $35 \div 5 =$ _____

c.

$18 \div 6 =$ _____ $42 \div 6 =$ _____ $24 \div 3 =$ _____ $64 \div 8 =$ _____

d.

$32 \div 8 =$ _____ $9 \div 3 =$ _____ $6 \div 2 =$ _____ $81 \div 9 =$ _____

e. $9\overline{)72}$ $5\overline{)15}$ $7\overline{)14}$ **h.** $9\overline{)36}$ $8\overline{)48}$ $5\overline{)5}$

f. $2\overline{)18}$ $8\overline{)72}$ $3\overline{)15}$ **i.** $4\overline{)20}$ $5\overline{)45}$ $6\overline{)48}$

g. $7\overline{)28}$ $6\overline{)24}$ $8\overline{)40}$ **j.** $9\overline{)18}$ $4\overline{)12}$ $9\overline{)27}$

Write the number sentence and label your answer.

a. John has 20¢. If donuts are 5¢ each, how many can he buy?

_____

John can buy _____ _____ .

b. Sue has 48¢. If cookies are 8¢ each, how many can she buy?

_____

Sue can buy _____ _____ .

c. The baker made 12 cake layers. He needs to make three cakes. How many layers will each cake have?

_____

Each will have _____ _____ .

d. The baker put 56 hot rolls in 8 rows. How many were in each row?

_____

Each row had _____ _____ .

e. The baker made 72 brownies. He put 9 rows of them on a tray. How many were in each row?

_____

Each row had _____ _____ .

f. If Jill buys 24 cream puffs and divides them equally into 4 bags, how many will be in each bag?

_____

Each bag will have _____ .

g. Bill has 49¢. If donut holes are 7¢ each, how many can he buy?

_____

Bill can buy _____ _____ .

Write the number sentence and label your answer.

a. There were 16 boy scouts. They slept in 8 tents. How many boys were in each tent?

_____

Each tent had _____ _____ .

b. There are 6 large tables in the mess hall. If there are 54 scouts, how many will sit at each table?

_____

There will be _____ _____ .

c. Seven groups of boy scouts went hiking. There were 42 boys. How many were in each group?

_____

Each group had _____ _____ .

d. If 32 girl scouts stayed in 4 cabins, how many were in each cabin?

_____

Each cabin had _____ _____ .

e. 63 girl scouts wanted to go boating. If there are 9 boats, how many girls will be in each boat?

_____

There will be _____ _____ .

f. If 25 scouts make 5 campfires, how many will sit at each campfire?

_____

_____ _____ will sit.

g. The arts and crafts leader can take groups of 9 scouts at a time. If 27 scouts sign up, how many groups would come?

_____

There would be _____ _____ .

Write each quotient
and remainder.

r. : remainder

How can you divide
19 apples equally
among 9 boys?

Make applesauce,
of course!

$$\begin{array}{r} 2 \ r.2 \\ \textbf{a.}\ 5\overline{)\ 12} \end{array}$$
$3\overline{)\ 10}$

b. $2\overline{)\ 17}$ $4\overline{)\ 38}$

c. $4\overline{)\ 33}$ $2\overline{)\ 9}$

d. $3\overline{)\ 23}$ $5\overline{)\ 41}$

e. $2\overline{)\ 11}$ $4\overline{)\ 10}$

f. $4\overline{)\ 25}$ $2\overline{)\ 17}$

g. $5\overline{)\ 33}$ $3\overline{)\ 20}$

h. $3\overline{)\ 28}$ $5\overline{)\ 9}$

i. $4\overline{)\ 29}$

j. $6\overline{)\ 14}$

k. $9\overline{)\ 75}$ $8\overline{)\ 75}$

l. $8\overline{)\ 13}$ $6\overline{)\ 50}$

m. $7\overline{)\ 37}$ $9\overline{)\ 89}$

n. $9\overline{)\ 30}$ $8\overline{)\ 30}$

o. $6\overline{)\ 11}$ $7\overline{)\ 19}$

p. $7\overline{)\ 57}$ $6\overline{)\ 55}$

q. $8\overline{)\ 58}$ $8\overline{)\ 66}$

r. $7\overline{)\ 50}$ $7\overline{)\ 48}$

s. $6\overline{)\ 39}$ $9\overline{)\ 46}$

t. $9\overline{)\ 55}$ $6\overline{)\ 33}$

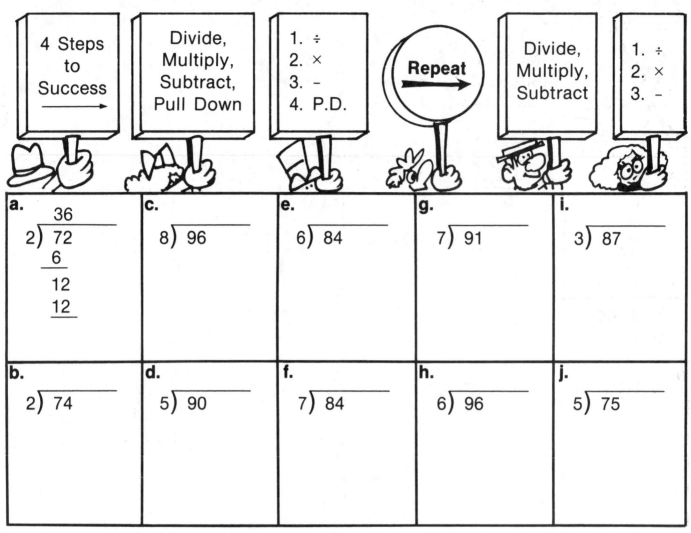

a.
$$2\overline{)72}$$
36
6
12
12

c.
$$8\overline{)96}$$

e.
$$6\overline{)84}$$

g.
$$7\overline{)91}$$

i.
$$3\overline{)87}$$

b.
$$2\overline{)74}$$

d.
$$5\overline{)90}$$

f.
$$7\overline{)84}$$

h.
$$6\overline{)96}$$

j.
$$5\overline{)75}$$

Find the quotients and remainders.

k.
$$5\overline{)68}$$

m.
$$2\overline{)71}$$

o.
$$6\overline{)79}$$

q.
$$7\overline{)94}$$

s.
$$4\overline{)75}$$

l.
$$3\overline{)74}$$

n.
$$6\overline{)94}$$

p.
$$3\overline{)47}$$

r.
$$7\overline{)99}$$

t.
$$6\overline{)88}$$

Name _____ Skill: Long division with 3-digit dividend

Divide, Multiply, Subtract, Pull Down
1. ÷
2. ×
3. –
4. P.D.

Repeat →

Divide, Multiply, Subtract
1. ÷
2. ×
3. –

```
    62 r.2
6) 374
   36
   14
   12
    2
```
Examples, Inc. !

Find the quotients.

b.   9) 756

d.   5) 390

f.   7) 196

a.   4) 304

c.   3) 201

e.   8) 512

g.   6) 222

Find the quotients and remainders.

h.   4) 187

j.   8) 339

l.   7) 268

n.   3) 176

i.   7) 400

k.   6) 215

m.   9) 319

o.   4) 107

$$6 \overline{) 4594} \quad \begin{array}{r} 765 \text{ r. } 4 \\ \hline \end{array}$$

42

39

36

34

30

4

Examples, Inc.

Find the quotients.

b. 3) 1728

d. 5) 4270

f. 7) 3759

a. 4) 3104

c. 8) 2144

e. 6) 1434

g. 9) 2205

Find the quotients and remainders.

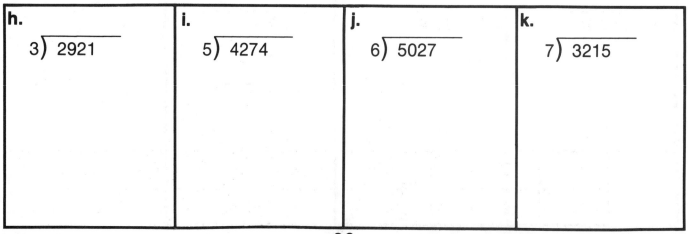

h. 3) 2921

i. 5) 4274

j. 6) 5027

k. 7) 3215

When is a bright idea
like a clock?

When __ __   __ __ __ __ __ __   __ __ __
      1 2   3 4 5 6 7 8   9 10 11 12

Directions: Solve each division problem.
Find the quotient and matching letter in
the code box below to answer the riddle.

1. 4)̄72	**2.** 3)̄1458	**3.** 7)̄161	**4.** 6)̄2916
5. 2)̄94	**6.** 9)̄162	**7.** 5)̄385	**8.** 4)̄2756
9. 5)̄115	**10.** 8)̄464	**11.** 6)̄150	**12.** 9)̄6201

18	23	25	47	58	77	486	689
i	**s**	**n**	**r**	**o**	**k**	**t**	**e**

Name _____

Review: Multiplication and division
word problems

Write the number sentence and label your answer.

d. Jack planted 3 rows of apple trees, with 6 trees in each row. How many apple trees does he have?

_____

Jack has _____ _____ .

a. Mary divided 10 peaches into 2 baskets. How many peaches are in each basket?

_____

There are _____ _____ .

e. If Sam planted 21 orange trees in 7 rows, how many trees are in each row?

_____

Each row had _____ _____ .

b. Sue had 9 baskets. If she put 7 apples in each one, how many apples did she pick?

_____

Sue picked _____ _____ .

f. Bill had 7 peach trees. He picked 4 good peaches from each tree. How many peaches did he have altogether?

_____

Bill had _____ _____ .

c. John divided 30 oranges equally among 6 friends. How many oranges did each friend get?

_____

Each friend got _____ _____ .

g. Betty has 63 apples to put into 7 baskets. How many apples did she put in each basket?

_____

Each basket had _____ _____ .

©Frank Schaffer Publications, Inc.   38   FS-2673 Math Workbook-Multiplication & Division

Name _____

Write the number sentence and label your answer.

a. Jim has 36¢. If candy bars are 9¢ each, how many can he buy?

_____

Jim can buy ____ _____ .

b. Sue has 7¢. Gumdrops are 1¢ each. How many can she buy?

_____

Sue can buy ____ _____ .

c. Candy mints are 3¢ each. If Nancy has 6¢, how many can she buy?

_____

Nancy can buy ____ _____ .

d. Bob wants to buy 6 candy bars. They are 9¢ each. How much money does he need?

_____

Bill needs _____ .

e. Bill bought 5 jawbreakers for 4¢ each. How much did he spend?

_____

Bill spent _____ .

f. Jack bought 2 packages of gum. There are 8 pieces of gum in each package. How many pieces did he have?

_____

Jack had ____ _____ .

g. The candy man has 8 jars of candy sticks. Each jar has 5 sticks of candy. How many are there altogether?

_____

There are ____ _____ .

Name _____

Write the number sentence and label your answer.

1. How much more will Bill spend than Sue if:

   a. Bill buys 5 oranges for 8¢ each? _____

   b. Sue buys 4 apples for 9¢ each? _____

   c. Bill will spend _____ more than Sue.

2. Which took less money to buy? (Circle a or b)

   a. Sue's 4 small cans of juice at 7¢ each. _____

   b. Bill's 3 cans of juice at 9¢ each. _____

   c. How much less money was it? _____

3. What is the cost per pear if:

   a. Bill spends 54¢ for 9 pears? _____

   b. Sue spends 28¢ for 4 pears? _____

   c. _____ spends _____ more per pear.

4. Who will spend less per lemon?

   a. Sue spends 64¢ on 8 lemons. _____

   b. Bill spends 25¢ on 5 lemons. _____

   c. _____ will spend _____ less per lemon.

5. How much difference is there in the total price?

   a. Bill buys 6 carrots for 7¢ each. _____

   b. Sue buys 5 potatoes for 9¢ each. _____

   c. There is _____ difference in price.

Name _____

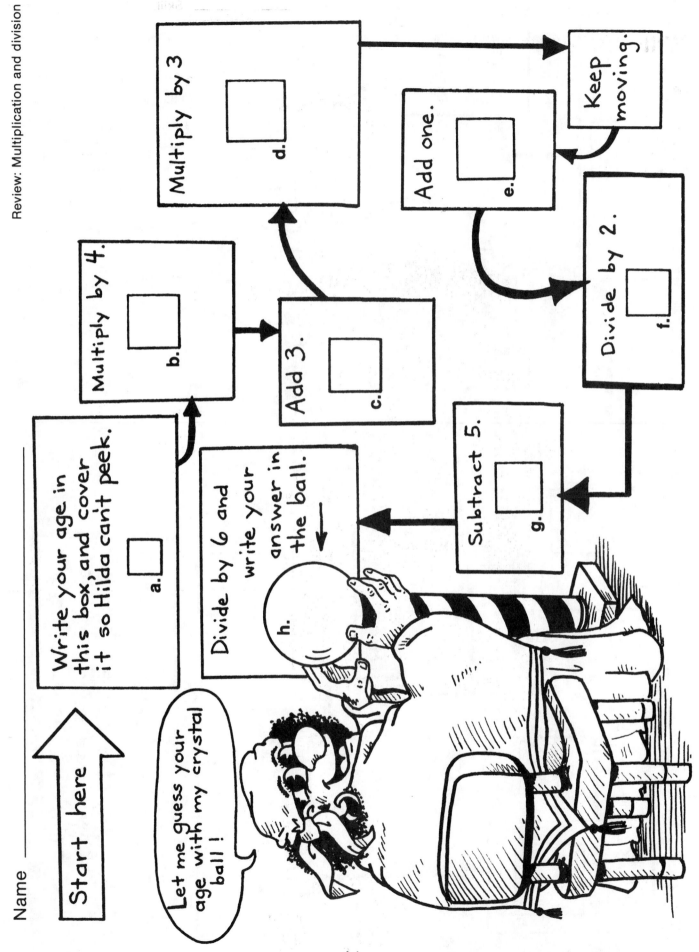

Start here

Write your age in this box, and cover it so Hilda can't peek.

a. ☐

Multiply by 4.

b. ☐

Add 3.

c. ☐

Multiply by 3

d. ☐

Add one.

e. ☐

Keep moving.

Divide by 2.

f. ☐

Subtract 5.

g. ☐

Divide by 6 and write your answer in the ball.

h.

Let me guess your age with my crystal ball!

Name

Name _____

Start here

a. Think of any counting number. Write it in the box.

b. Add 5.

c. Multiply by 5.

d. Add 3.

e. Multiply by two.

f. Subtract ten times your original number.

g. Divide by 8.

I can turn any counting number into a seven!

How does he do it?

43

Name _____

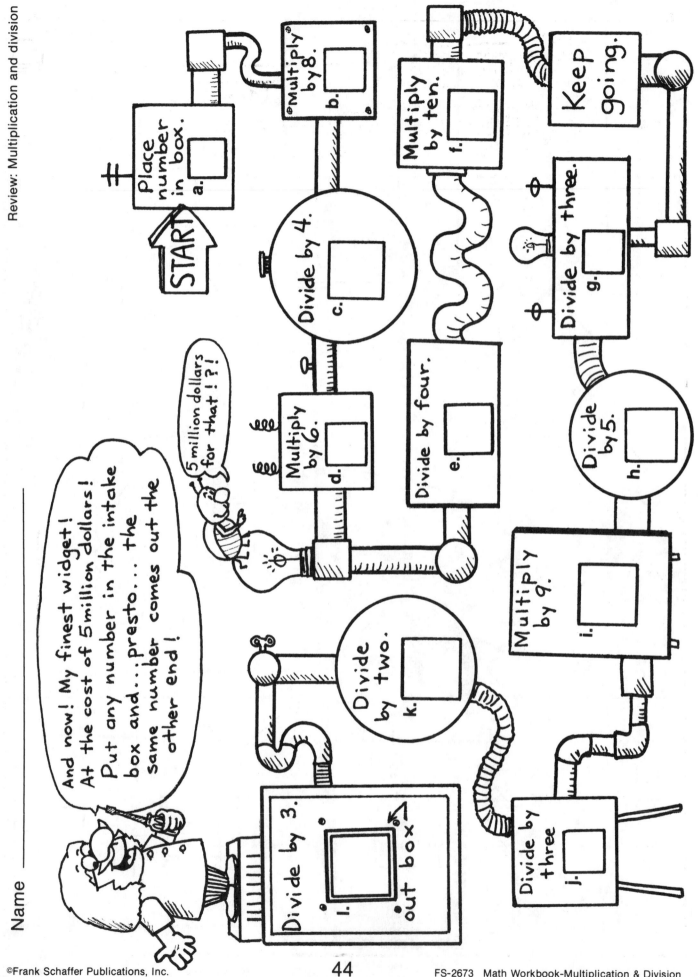

FS-2673 Math Workbook-Multiplication & Division

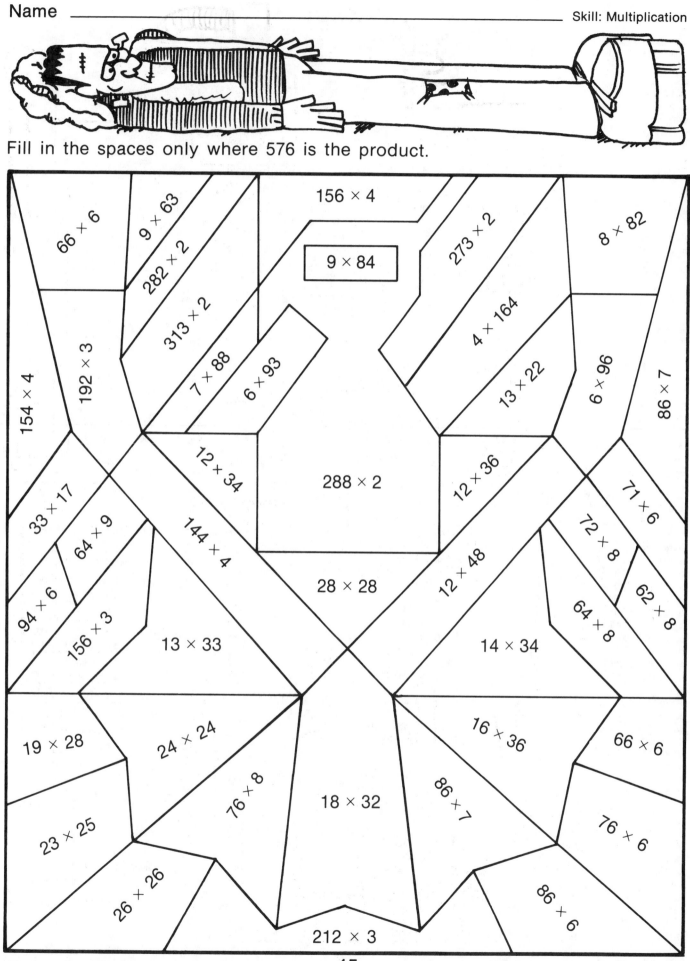

Fill in the spaces only where 576 is the product.

Answers

Page One
a. 6, 8, 14
b. 16, 8, 10
c. 14, 16, 10
d. 2, 4, 18
e. 0, 14, 16
f. 6, 12, 0
g. 18, 8, 10
h. 0, 14, 8
i. 10, 6, 14
j. 2, 18, 12
k. 12, 4, 16
l. 0, 16, 6

Page Two
a. 6, 18, 6, 21
b. 18, 12, 0, 27
c. 3, 24, 21, 15
d. 9, 24, 27
e. 0, 15, 6, 3
f. 21, 3, 12, 9
g. 6, 27, 18, 3
h. 12, 27, 12, 0
i. 18, 24, 12, 15
j. 21, 0, 15, 24

Page Three
a. 24, 12, 0
b. 16, 8, 28
c. 20, 36, 32
d. 20, 36, 32
e. 36, 0, 24
f. 12, 4, 36
g. 0, 36
h. 24, 0, 12, 32, 36, 8
i. 4, 20, 24, 28, 16, 12
j. 4, 0, 36, 32, 28, 20

Page Four
a. 10, 0, 45, 30, 45
b. 20, 10, 5, 15, 5
c. 35, 20, 35, 0, 40
d. 40, 30, 25, 30, 15
e. 15, 0, 20, 40
f. 35, 10, 30, 45
g. 0, 15, 5, 30
h. 30, 25, 5, 45
i. 30, 40, 25, 35
j. 15, 20, 45, 40

Page Five
a. 12, 24, 42
b. 6, 30, 54
c. 18, 36, 6
d. 42, 30, 54
e. 0, 18, 24
f. 36, 30, 42, 0, 12, 48
g. 18, 12, 24, 54, 6
h. 48, 24, 6, 18, 54, 42

Page Six
a. 14
b. 14, 42
c. 49, 21
d. 35
e. 63
f. 0
g. 7
h. 56
i. 35, 28
j. 56, 63
k. 35, 0, 28
l. 0, 42, 14
m. 56, 63, 7
n. 28, 21, 56
o. 63, 28, 14
p. 49, 42, 35

Page Seven
a. 16, 0, 56
b. 32, 16, 0
c. 48, 72, 32
d. 56, 48, 8
e. 64, 24, 40
f. 72, 64
g. 24, 32, 0, 32
h. 48, 16, 56, 8
i. 40, 48, 72, 56

Page Eight
a. 36, 63
b. 72, 27
c. 0, 54
d. 54
e. 18
f. 45
g. 9
h. 63
i. 0
j. 27, 36
k. 45, 9
l. 81, 54
m. 0, 27, 63, 54
n. 72, 18, 72, 81
o. 45, 36, 0, 36
p. 63, 54, 9, 27
q. 18, 45, 63, 27
r. 72, 0, 81, 54

Page Nine
a. 32, 4, 54, 35, 63, 72
b. 12, 27, 63, 12, 14, 20
c. 18, 35, 16, 18, 40, 49
d. 48, 24, 8, 6, 48, 18
e. 21, 9, 28, 64, 45, 63
f. 8, 25, 0, 15, 72, 28
g. 42, 32, 27, 24, 48, 40
h. 0, 36, 21, 56, 30, 14
i. 45, 24, 54, 16, 16, 56

Page Ten
a. 6, 42, 27
b. 14, 18, 12
c. 36, 8, 28
d. 30, 72, 49
e. 64, 35, 18
f. 48, 0, 56
g. 42, 0, 18
h. 25, 24, 12
i. 54, 40, 21
j. 20, 63, 24
k. 15, 36, 72
l. 81, 32, 9

Page Eleven
a. $3 \times 8 = 24$, 24 legs
b. $5 \times 6 = 30$, 30 legs
c. $8 \times 4 = 32$, 32 arms
d. $6 \times 3 = 18$, 18 legs
e. $3 \times 4 = 12$, 12 legs
f. $2 \times 7 = 14$, 14 feet
g. $0 \times 3 = 0$, 0 legs

Page Twelve
a. $9 \times 3 = 27$, 27 outs
b. $4 \times 9 = 36$, 36 people
c. $5 \times 9 = 45$, 45 points
d. $6 \times 8 = 48$, 48 points
e. $8 \times 7 = 56$, 56 laps
f. $6 \times 4 = 24$, 24 miles
g. $6 \times 7 = 42$, 42 games

Page Thirteen
a. 69, 148, 190
b. 76, 430, 81
c. 138, 80, 98
d. 133, 304, 384
e. 336, 135, 288
f. 98, 260, 90
g. 364, 744, 432
h. 378, 400, 168
i. 399, 171, 420

Page Fourteen
a. 1,245; 1,974; 1,640; 952; 468
b. 4,320; 1,104; 1,587; 380; 836
c. 3,740; 1,458; 2,028; 1,795; 1,816
d. 3,850; 3,102; 1,152; 3,704; 2,926
e. 8,496; 2,156; 2,328; 4,044; 8,010
f. 2,616; 7,884; 5,454; 3,241; 4,864

Page Fifteen

a.

200	282	332	72
+1000	+2350	+2490	+3240
1200	2632	2822	3312

b.

378	350	568	567	342
+1680	+4000	+3550	+4410	+760
2058	4350	4118	4977	1102

c.

168	420	108	558	546
+1680	+1680	+1350	+1860	+3900
1848	2100	1458	2418	4446

d.

315	536	648	00	184
+1350	+5360	+2160	+4150	+3220
1665	5896	2808	4150	3404

Page Sixteen

a.

4718	2250	4585	1626	2436
+13480	+27000	+18340	+37940	+8120
18198	29250	22925	39566	10556

b.

3412	1384	7216	1800	3805
+59710	+17300	+36080	+12000	+15220
63122	18684	43296	13800	19025

c.

4718	3232	3888	2940	1656
+13480	+24240	+21600	+51450	+18630
18198	27472	25488	54390	20286

d.

2616	6176	2763	8208	5488
+16350	+30880	+15350	+63840	+41160
18966	37056	18113	72048	46648

Page Seventeen
a. $6 \times 7 = 42$, $3 \times 7 = 21$, $8 \times 7 = 56$, $4 \times 7 = 28$
b. $7 \times 7 = 49$, $9 \times 7 = 63$, $11 \times 7 = 77$, $10 \times 7 = 70$
c. $12 \times 7 = 84$, $20 \times 7 = 140$, $0 \times 7 = 0$, $700 \times 7 = 4,900$
d. $100 \times 7 = 700$, $1 \times 7 = 7$, $30 \times 7 = 210$, $40 \times 7 = 280$

Page Eighteen
a. $6 \times 8 = 48$, $5 \times 8 = 40$, $8 \times 8 = 64$, $4 \times 8 = 32$
b. $7 \times 8 = 56$, $9 \times 8 = 72$, $11 \times 8 = 88$, $10 \times 8 = 80$
c. $12 \times 8 = 96$, $30 \times 8 = 240$, $0 \times 8 = 0$, $700 \times 8 = 5,600$
d. $100 \times 8 = 800$, $1 \times 8 = 8$, $30 \times 8 = 240$, $40 \times 8 = 320$

Answers

Page Nineteen
a. 5 × $9 = $45
b. 8 × $9 = $72
c. 7 × $9 = $63
d. 6 × $9 = $54
e. 9 × $9 = $81
f. 4 × $9 = $36
g. 4 × $7 = $28
h. 8 × $7 = $56
i. 9 × $7 = $63
j. 6 × $7 = $42
k. 5 × $7 = $35
l. 6 × $8 = $48
m. 9 × $8 = $72
n. 7 × $8 = $56
o. 4 × $8 = $32
p. 8 × $8 = $64
q. 0 × $8 = 0

Page Twenty
a. 5 × 59¢ = $2.95
b. 2 × 37¢ = 74¢
c. 3 × 59¢ = $1.77
d. 4 × 78¢ = $3.12
e. 2 × 59¢ = $1.18
f. 9 × 37¢ = $3.33
g. 6 × 37¢ = $2.22
h. 2 × 78¢ = $1.56
i. 6 × 78¢ = $4.68

Page Twenty-One
a. 2, 5, 8
b. 2, 1, 2
c. 9, 2, 5
d. 2, 6, 2
e. 2, 3, 5
f. 4, 2, 2
g. 2, 2, 9
h. 1, 2, 3
i. 6, 2, 2, 2, 2
j. 8, 2, 3, 2
k. 2, 2, 5, 1
l. 9, 2, 4, 2

Page Twenty-Two
a. 9, 3, 3
b. 8, 3, 3
c. 5, 3, 3
d. 3, 7, 3
e. 4, 2, 6
f. 4, 3, 9, 3, 6
g. 2, 3, 8, 1, 3
h. 7, 3, 3, 3, 3

Page Twenty-Three
a. 4, 8
b. 4, 2
c. 7, 9
d. 5, 4
e. 6, 4
f. 4, 4
g. 4, 6
h. 1, 4
i. 2, 4, 4
j. 4, 4, 3
k. 9, 4, 4
l. 2, 8, 4
m. 4, 1, 7

Page Twenty-Four
a. 9, 5
b. 5, 2
c. 5, 8
d. 5, 3
e. 3, 5
f. 6, 5
g. 5, 5
h. 1, 4
i. 7, 5
j. 5, 5
k. 5, 4, 7
l. 9, 5, 5
m. 6, 5, 5
n. 2, 5, 5
o. 5, 1, 8
p. 5, 3, 9

Page Twenty-Five
a. 3
b. 6
c. 9, 6, 4
d. 2, 6, 6
e. 8, 6, 6
f. 1, 6, 6
g. 7, 6, 3
h. 5, 6, 6, 4
i. 6, 6, 4, 2
j. 3, 6, 6, 8
k. 2, 5, 6, 6, 1, 6
l. 6, 9, 6, 4, 6, 2

Page Twenty-Six
a. 9, 7, 5
b. 7, 4, 7, 8
c. 7, 7, 2, 3
d. 1, 7, 7, 2
e. 7, 1, 6, 7
f. 7, 7, 9, 7
g. 7, 5, 4, 7
h. 2, 8, 7, 7

Page Twenty-Seven
a. 8, 4, 8
b. 8, 1, 8
c. 8, 7, 8
d. 3, 8, 6
e. 5, 2, 8
f. 9, 8
g. 8
h. 8, 5, 8, 1, 3
i. 8, 8, 4, 8, 9
j. 8, 6, 8, 7, 8
k. 8, 8, 2, 8, 8

Page Twenty-Eight
a. 8, 5, 2, 9
b. 3, 9, 4, 9
c. 1, 9, 9, 7
d. 9, 9, 6, 2
e. 9, 7, 9, 5
f. 9, 9, 1, 9, 9
g. 6, 9, 9, 9, 2
h. 9, 4, 9, 5, 9
i. 1, 2, 9, 8, 3

Page Twenty-Nine
a. O X X
X X O
O X O
winner: X (2)
b. X X O
X O X
O O X
winner: O (6)
c. O X X
X O X
X O O
winner: O (9)
d. O X O
X X O
X O O
winner: O (8)
e. X X O
X O X
X X O
winner: X (9)

Page Thirty
a. 4, 2, 1, 3
b. 5, 5, 5, 7
c. 3, 7, 8, 8
d. 4, 3, 3, 9
e. 8, 3, 2
f. 9, 9, 5
g. 4, 4, 5
h. 4, 6, 1
i. 5, 9, 8
j. 2, 3, 3

Page Thirty-One
a. 20¢ ÷ 5¢ = 4, 4 donuts
b. 48¢ ÷ 8¢ = 6, 6 cookies
c. 12 ÷ 3 = 4, 4 layers
d. 56 ÷ 8 = 7, 7 hot rolls
e. 72 ÷ 9 = 8, 8 brownies
f. 24 ÷ 4 = 6, 6 cream puffs
g. 49¢ ÷ 7¢ = 7, 7 donut holes

Page Thirty-Two
a. 16 ÷ 8 = 2, 2 boy scouts
b. 54 ÷ 6 = 9, 9 scouts
c. 42 ÷ 7 = 6, 6 boy scouts
d. 32 ÷ 4 = 8, 8 girl scouts
e. 63 ÷ 9 = 7, 7 girl scouts
f. 25 ÷ 5 = 5, 5 scouts
g. 27 ÷ 9 = 3, 3 groups

Page Thirty-Three
a. 2 r. 2, 3 r. 1
b. 8 r. 1, 9 r. 2
c. 8 r. 1, 4 r. 1
d. 7 r. 2, 8 r. 1
e. 5 r. 1, 2 r. 2
f. 6 r. 1, 8 r. 1
g. 6 r. 3, 6 r. 2
h. 9 r. 1, 1 r. 4
i. 7 r. 1
j. 2 r. 2
k. 8 r. 3, 9 r. 3
l. 1 r. 5, 8 r. 2
m. 5 r. 2, 9 r. 8
n. 3 r. 3, 3 r. 6
o. 1 r. 5, 2 r. 5
p. 8 r. 1, 9 r. 1
q. 7 r. 2, 8 r. 2
r. 7 r. 1, 6 r. 6
s. 6 r. 3, 5 r. 1
t. 6 r. 1, 5 r. 3

Page Thirty-Four
a. 36
b. 37
c. 12
d. 18
e. 14
f. 12
g. 13
h. 16
i. 29
j. 15
k. 13 r. 3
l. 24 r. 2
m. 35 r. 1
n. 15 r. 4
o. 13 r. 1
p. 15 r. 2
q. 13 r. 3
r. 14 r. 1
s. 18 r. 3
t. 14 r. 4

Page Thirty-Five
a. 76
b. 84
c. 67
d. 78
e. 64
f. 28
g. 37
h. 46 r. 3
i. 57 r. 1
j. 42 r. 3
k. 35 r. 5
l. 38 r. 2
m. 35 r. 4
n. 58 r. 2
o. 26 r. 3

       FS-2673 Math Workbook-Multiplication & Division

Answers

Page Thirty-Six

a. 776

b. 576

c. 268

d. 854

e. 239

f. 537

g. 245

h. 973 r. 2

i. 854 r. 4

j. 837 r. 5

k. 459 r. 2

Page Thirty-Seven

<u>i</u> <u>t</u>   <u>s</u> <u>t</u> <u>r</u> <u>i</u> <u>k</u> <u>e</u> <u>s</u>   <u>o</u> <u>n</u> <u>e</u>
1 2   3 4 5 6 7 8 9   10 11 12

1. 18

2. 486

3. 23

4. 486

5. 47

6. 18

7. 77

8. 689

9. 23

10. 58

11. 25

12. 689

Page Thirty-Eight

a. $10 \div 2 = 5$, 5 peaches

b. $9 \times 7 = 63$, 63 apples

c. $30 \div 6 = 5$, 5 oranges

d. $3 \times 6 = 18$, 18 apple trees

e. $21 \div 7 = 3$, 3 trees

f. $7 \times 4 = 28$, 28 peaches

g. $63 \div 7 = 9$, 9 apples

Page Thirty-Nine

a. 36¢ ÷ 9¢ = 4, 4 candy bars

b. 7¢ ÷ 1¢ = 7, 7 gumdrops

c. 6¢ ÷ 3¢ = 2, 2 mints

d. 6×9¢ = 54¢, 54¢

e. 5×4¢ = 20¢, 20¢

f. $2 \times 8 = 16$, 16 pieces

g. $8 \times 5 = 40$, 40 candy sticks

Page Forty

1. a. 5×8¢ = 40¢

b. 4×9¢ = 36¢

c. 40¢ − 36¢ = 4¢

2. a. 4×7¢ = 28¢

(b.) 3×9¢ = 27¢

c. 1¢

3. a. 54¢ ÷ 9 = 6¢

b. 28¢ ÷ 4 = 7¢

c. Sue, 1¢

4. a. 64¢ ÷ 8 = 8¢

b. 25¢ ÷ 5 = 5¢

c. Bill, 3¢

5. a. 6×7¢ = 42¢

b. 5×9¢ = 45¢

c. 3¢

Page Forty-One

Answers vary.

Page Forty-Two

Answers vary.

Page Forty-Three

Answers vary.

Page Forty-Four

Answers vary.

Page Forty-Five

FS-2673 Math Workbook-Multiplication & Division